ASSOULINE
FALL 2017

Welcome

Assouline was created as the first luxury brand on culture. We love and believe in books more than anything else, but have also extended our vision to create all that can be expected in a chic and contemporary library, from special editions to luxury gift items, unique library accessories, furniture pieces, and objets d'art.

Our digital world goes faster than ever and nothing remains of it, but books are the solid part of our past and present. They are a matter of intellect and emotion, of heritage and innovation, of pleasure and beauty.

We hope you enjoy our selection for Fall 2017 and bring as much of our world as possible into yours.

Prosper and Martine Assouline
Founders, Chairman & CEO

Assouline is dedicated to making each of our books a complete experience. Objects and curios pictured in *Ottoman Chic* can be purchased at Maison Assouline, and food and drink inspired by our titles can be enjoyed at the Swans Bar.

FALL 2017

"A ROOM WITHOUT BOOKS IS LIKE A BODY WITHOUT A SOUL."

CICERO

1
Ultimate Collection

ANDY WARHOL · 14
The Impossible Collection

GOLF · 18
The Impossible Collection
The 100 Most Legendary Courses in the World

THE IMPOSSIBLE COLLECTION OF WINE · 22
The 100 Most Exceptional Vintages of the 20th Century

BARBIE · 24

THE HIDDEN COLLECTION · 26

FERNANDO BOTERO · 28

2
Legends Collection

BULGARI *The Joy of Gems* · 32

PIERRE CARDIN · 36

JEAN-MICHEL FRANK · 38

DIOR BY CHRISTIAN DIOR · 40

DIOR BY YVES SAINT LAURENT · 42

DIOR BY MARC BOHAN · 43

MARIA BY CALLAS *In Her Own Words* · 44

DE GRISOGONO *Daring Creativity* · 46

CANADA GOOSE *Greatness Is Out There* · 50

BE EXTRAORDINARY *The Spirit of Bentley* · 51

SEVAN BIÇAKÇI *Time* · 52

3
Classics Collection

DONALD · 56

GUY BOURDIN *Image Maker* · 62

THE ARCTIC MELT · 64
Images of a Disappearing Landscape

ASPEN STYLE · 66

IBIZA BOHEMIA · 68

SANTIAGO CALATRAVA *Oculus* · 70

THE BOSPHORUS LIFE · 72

ART HOUSE *The Collaboration of Chara Schreyer & Gary Hutton* · 74

REFLECTIONS *In Conversation with Today's Artists by Matt Black* · 74

GIACOBETTI · 75

BEAUMARLY PARIS · 76

CHIC STAYS *Condé Nast Traveller's Favourite People on Their Favourite Places* · 77

THE ITALIAN DREAM *Wine, Heritage, Soul* · 78

ETERNALLY RITZ · 83

ASHFORD CASTLE · 87

JOURNEY BY DESIGN *Katharine Pooley* · 87

VENETIAN CHIC · 87

4
Icons Collection

THE LUXURY COLLECTION · 92
Global Epicurean

TRAVELS WITH CHUFY · 93
Confidential Destinations by Sofía Sanchez de Betak

COCKTAIL CHAMELEON · 94

TRANSFORM · 96
60 Makeup Looks by Toni Malt

COVA · 97

5
Mémoire Collection

CHAUMET *Photography, Arts, Fetes* · 98

CHANEL *Fashion, Fine Jewelry, Perfume* · 98

DIOR *Couture, Fine Jewellery, Perfume* · 98

Miscellaneous

DINNER WITH GEORGIA O'KEEFFE · 85
Recipes, Art & Landscape

ALAIN ELKANN INTERVIEWS · 86

THE ART OF @BARBIESTYLE · 88

POKER *The Ultimate Book* · 100

BACKLIST · 104 / INDEX · 131
STORES · 138 / CREDITS · 140

Ultimate Collection

AT ASSOULINE, FINE CRAFTSMANSHIP IS OUR PHILOSOPHY. THE ULTIMATE COLLECTION HERALDS A RETURN TO THE LUXURY, CARE, AND MYSTIQUE OF A FINE HANDCRAFTED BOOK. EACH LIMITED-EDITION VOLUME IS METICULOUSLY HANDMADE, AND EVERY PAGE BEARS THE UNIQUE IMPRINT OF THE ARTISAN.

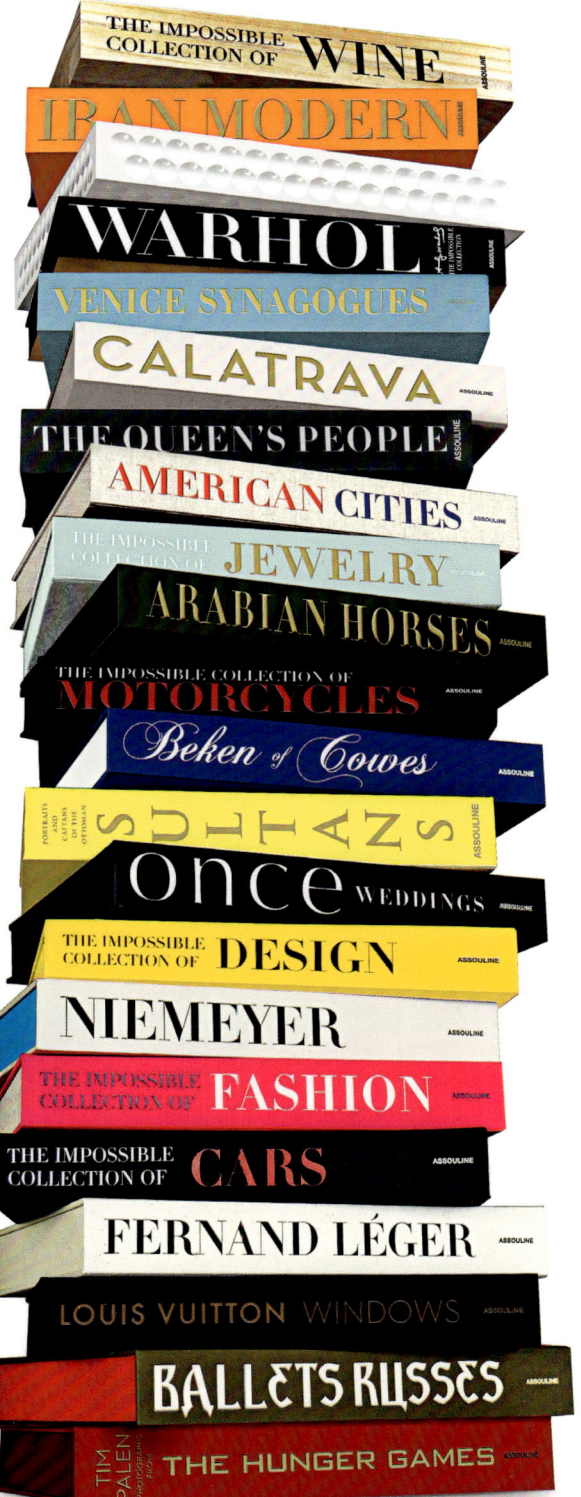

NEW

Ultimate Collection

ANDY WARHOL
THE IMPOSSIBLE COLLECTION

EVEN WARHOL CONNOISSEURS WILL FIND AN ELEMENT OF SURPRISE IN THESE PAGES.

Andy Warhol's explosive pop art and sharp commentary on advertising and celebrity culture are renowned and deeply relevant even decades after their creation. In this evocative volume, Warhol expert and former Andy Warhol Museum director Eric Shiner curates the 100 quintessential unique works that define the evolution of this illustrious artist, creating a stunning compendium of pieces that could simply never all be acquired by a single collector. Casual art lovers know *Campbell's Soup Cans* and the *Marilyn Diptych*, but *Andy Warhol: The Impossible Collection* goes deeper, revealing and revisiting some less ubiquitous yet equally powerful paintings, prints, sculpture, films, and photography from Warhol's astonishing oeuvre.

Text by Eric Shiner | 14 x 17 in – 35.5 x 42 cm | 172 pages | 100 illustrations | 6 gatefolds | handcrafted limited edition in a luxury clamshell case | ISBN: 9781614286271 | $845 – €850 – £650

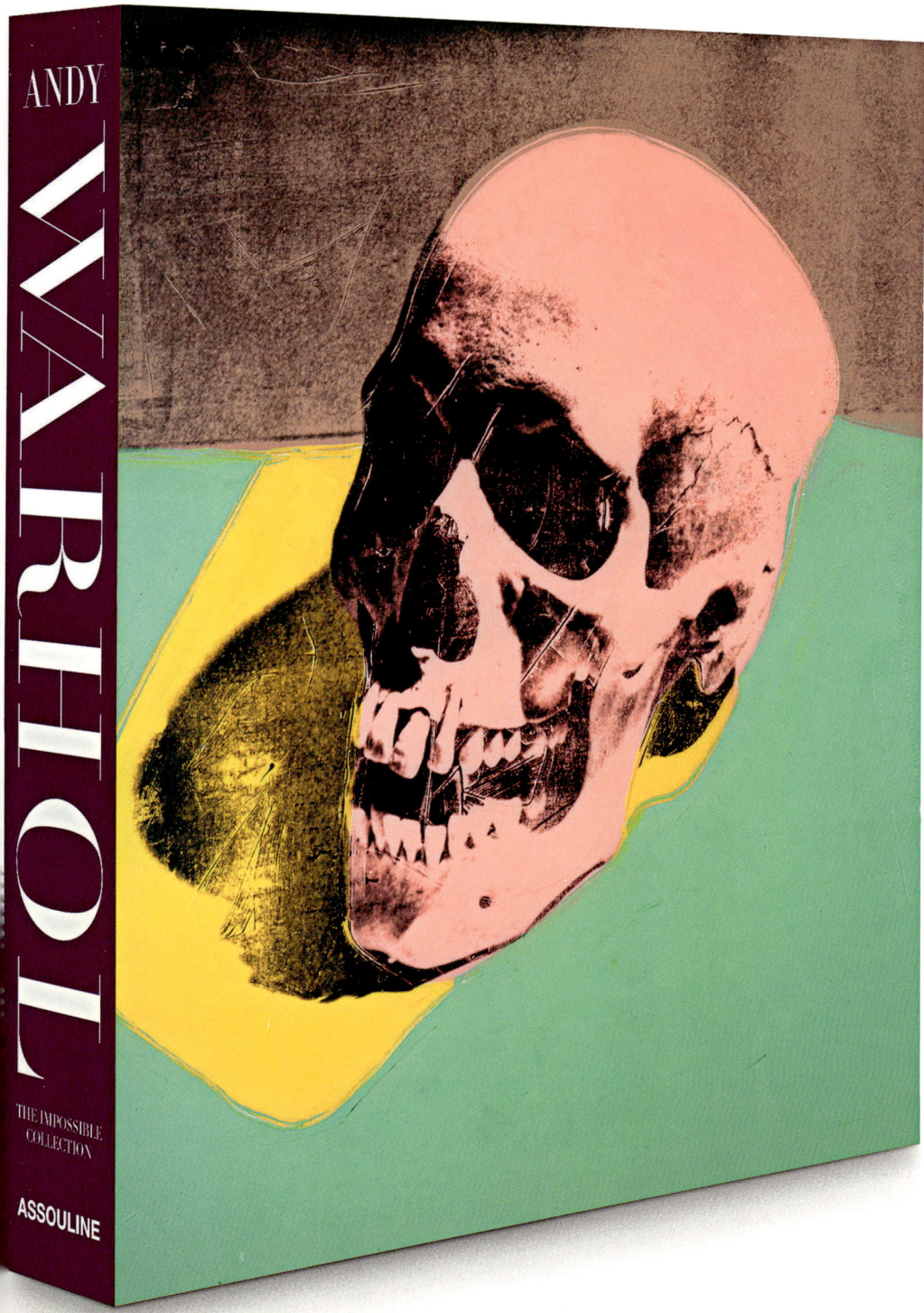

ilkscreen painting that riffs on the concept of highbrow art as rare and cov
industry as his source material, Warhol places image after image a
t the work with both respect and a heavy dose of humor.

1962 / Eighteen
S&H GREEN STAMPS

Like most depression-era families, the Warholas collected S&H Green Stamps that could be tra[ded in a] national promotional campaign for grocery stores. This painting, made with hand-carved rub[ber stamps, hints at a] future of things to come in its nearly blank arrangement, with only a few stamps in the upper [left corner. Warhol's] future and career filling up the blank region as he collects accolades and atte[ntion.]

Ultimate Collection

GOLF
THE IMPOSSIBLE COLLECTION
THE 100 MOST LEGENDARY COURSES IN THE WORLD

In this most recent addition to Assouline's highly covetable and lauded Ultimate Collection, George Peper, former editor in chief of *Golf* magazine and 2016 PGA Lifetime Achievement Award winner for Journalism, takes readers on an incomparable golf journey as he travels the world detailing the 100 most significant, historically noteworthy, and architecturally paramount courses. Describing intricate holes that have confounded the game's best, revisiting tournaments that have made and broken champions, and elucidating the unique and truly special characteristics of each course makes Peper the perfect golf partner as he walks readers through the clubhouses, the fairways, and the bunkers. From greens as old and hallowed as St Andrews to courses celebrating their first anniversary such as Nova Scotia's Cabot Cliffs, from the island mountain course of China's Shanqin Bay to the Hamptons' Maidstone Club, *Golf: The Impossible Collection* is an unequivocal sensory treat for the golf fanatic, or the perfect feast to feed the wanderlust simmering in all of us.

By George Peper | 14 x 17 in - 35.5 x 42 cm | 200 pages | 130 illustrations | handcrafted limited edition in a luxury case with white gloss finish | ISBN: 9781614286530 | $945 - €950 - £750

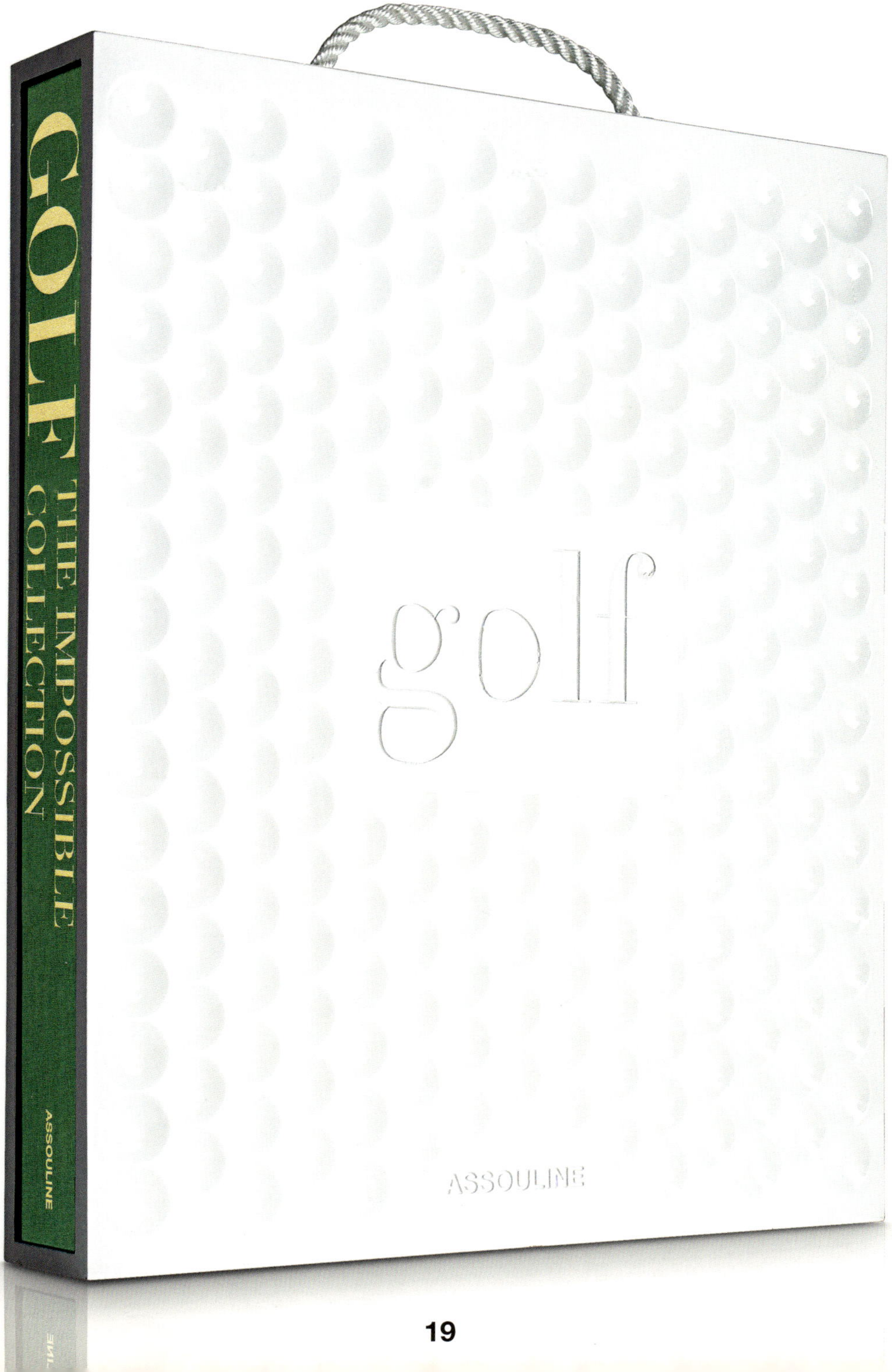
GOLF THE IMPOSSIBLE COLLECTION
ASSOULINE
golf
ASSOULINE

"GOLF IS THE CLOSEST GAME TO THE GAME WE CALL LIFE. YOU GET BAD BREAKS FROM GOOD SHOTS; YOU GET GOOD BREAKS FROM BAD SHOTS, BUT YOU HAVE TO PLAY THE BALL WHERE IT LIES."

BOBBY JONES, PROFESSIONAL GOLFER

Ultimate Collection

THE IMPOSSIBLE COLLECTION OF WINE

"IN THIS ULTRA-LUXE WINE COLLECTOR'S COMPENDIUM, SOMMELIER ENRICO BERNARDO OFFERS HIS ALL-STAR LIST OF WINE FOR POSTERITY— A FANTASY CELLAR, IF YOU WILL."

WINE SPECTATOR

In this stunning Ultimate Collection volume, Enrico Bernardo, the world's best sommelier, imagines the perfect cellar filled with the most exceptional wines of the twentieth century: *The Impossible Collection of Wine*. Weighing the virtues of rarity, terroir, taste, and historical mystique, Bernardo's is a list any connoisseur could only dream of. Bernardo celebrates the most exquisite vintages from around the globe—from the 1928 Krug Collection Champagne to the 1951 Penfolds Grange Bin 95 to the 1973 Stag's Leap Estate SLV—inviting the reader on a journey through history to savor an impossible collection.

By Enrico Bernardo, foreword by Michael Broadbent
14 x 17 in – 35.5 x 42 cm | 200 pages | 150 illustrations
handcrafted limited edition in a wooden crate
ISBN: 9781614284710 | $845 – €850 – £650
also available in French
($945 after January 1, 2018)

FEBRUARY 2018

Ultimate Collection

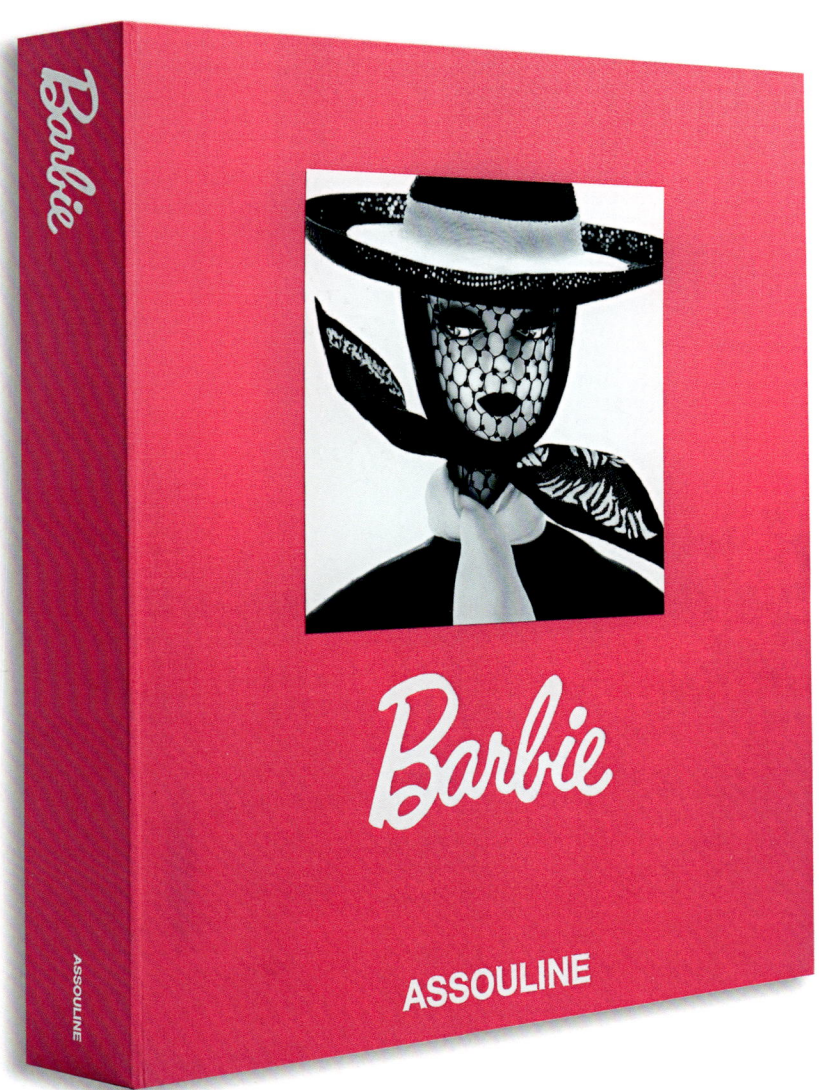

Far more than just a plastic toy, Barbie mirrors the evolution of modern culture, and provides the ultimate canvas for artistic and fashion inspiration, from Andy Warhol to Karl Lagerfeld. This beautiful Ultimate Collection volume showcases this modern cultural icon with exquisitely detailed photographs, vividly illustrating the many facets of Barbie as a fashionable figure of glamour, adventure, and fun.

Text by Yona Zeldis McDonough | 14 x 17 in – 35.5 x 42 cm | 144 pages | 80 illustrations | 4 gatefolds handcrafted limited edition in a luxury clamshell case | ISBN: 9782759403110 | $845 – €850 – £650

"BARBIE IS BOTH MIRROR AND MODEL, REFLECTION AND PIONEER. AS LONG AS THERE IS A NEED FOR THE KIND OF MAGICALLY LIBERATING, OPEN-ENDED FANTASY SHE NOT ONLY ALLOWS BUT INSPIRES, BARBIE WILL BE WITH US."

FEBRUARY 2018

Ultimate Collection

THE HIDDEN COLLECTION

Empress Farah Pahlavi dedicated her life to serving the Iranian people. With a keen eye—and working with Sotheby's, Christie's, and the Met— the Empress was able to amass one of the world's greatest collections of modern art for her country, including works by van Gogh, Picasso, Bacon, and de Kooning. Then, in 1979, the unimaginable happened, and the Iran that emerged changed everything. *The Hidden Collection* uncovers the lost story of Pahlavi's amazing journey from Empress to exile, and illuminates the near-forgotten collection of contemporary art she left behind.

Foreword by Empress Farah Pahlavi, text by Viola Raikhel-Bolot and Miranda Darling | 14 x 17 in - 35.5 x 42 cm | 200 pages | 100 illustrations handcrafted limited edition in a luxury clamshell case | ISBN: 9781614286349 $845 – €850 – £650

Ultimate Collection

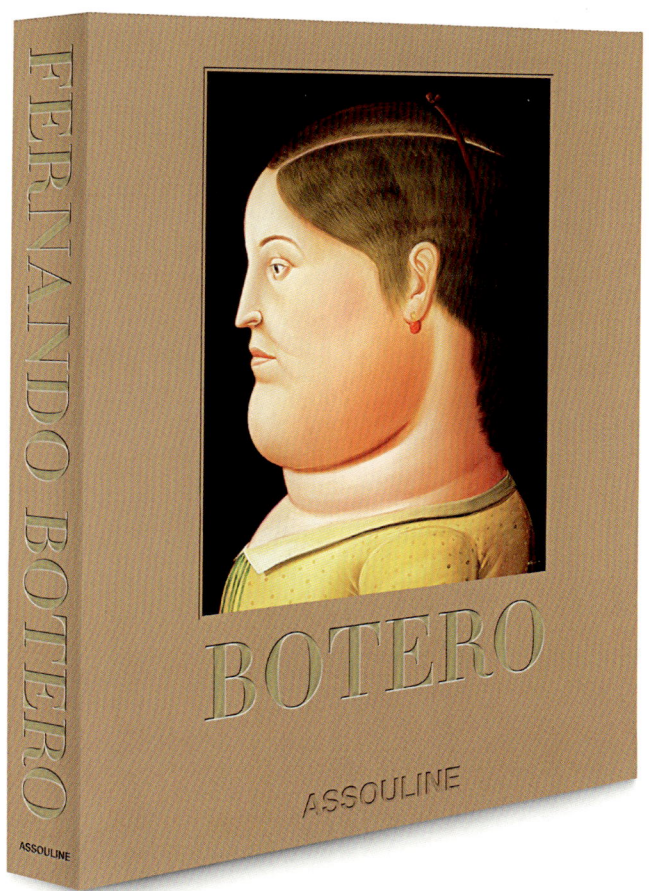

"ART SHOULD AIM TO TRANSCEND LIFE AND TO ELEVATE SPIRITUALLY."

FERNANDO BOTERO

Few artists have created a world as distinctive as that of Botero, who enjoys an exceptional position as one of the most successful contemporary artists. This spectacular handcrafted Ultimate Collection volume includes previously unpublished works and was curated in collaboration with the renowned artist himself from among Botero's most important works from each period of his singular oeuvre.

Text by Cristina Carrillo de Albornoz Fisac | 14 x 17 in - 35.5 x 42 cm | 160 pages | 100 illustrations
Handcrafted limited edition in a linen clamshell case | ISBN: 9781614284734 | $845 - €850 - £650

Legends Collection

ASSOULINE'S LEGENDS COLLECTION ARE REFINED HARDCOVER TOMES HOUSED IN THEIR OWN ELEGANT SLIPCASES. THESE TITLES ARE THE AUTHORITY ON THEIR SUBJECTS, CELEBRATING MYTHIC ERAS, ARTISTS, AND HIGH SOCIETY. FIT FOR ROYALTY, THEY ARE INSPIRED BY TASTEMAKERS ACROSS THE CENTURIES, AND ARE ESSENTIAL TO THE CULTURALLY INCLINED INFLUENCERS OF TODAY.

NEW

BVLGARI
ROMA

THE JOY OF GEMS
MAGNIFICENT HIGH JEWELRY CREATIONS

"BULGARI'S WONDROUS COLLECTIONS OF HIGH JEWELRY ARE UNIQUE WORKS OF ART CENTERED ON THE RAREST, MOST BEAUTIFUL GEMSTONES, EARTH'S PRECIOUS NATURAL TREASURES."

Bulgari's exquisite high jewelry creations are conjured from the vibrant color, life, and light of exceptional gemstones, infused with an innate Roman sense of history, and invigorated with an audacious spirit of modernity. The very soul of the Eternal City is encapsulated in the extraordinary colored gems, each specially selected for its charisma and vivacity, that have become the signature of Bulgari style. This luxurious slipcase edition is brought to glorious life through a spectacular array of magnificent Bulgari jewels.

Text by Vivienne Becker, original photography by Laziz Hamani | 12 x 15.5 in – 30 x 39 cm | 300 pages 200 illustrations | hardcover in a luxury slipcase | ISBN: 9781614286158 | $250 – €250 – £195

"GEMS BUILD VISUAL INTENSITY AND EMOTION, FORMING AN INTEGRAL PART OF THE STORYTELLING OF EACH HIGH JEWELRY CREATION, GENERATING A RHYTHMIC FLOW OF LIGHT, LEADING THE EYE AND HEART THROUGH A LANDSCAPE OF COLOR AND TEXTURE, ALWAYS SURPRISING, YET ALWAYS UNMISTAKABLY, INIMITABLY BULGARI."

NEW

pierre cardin

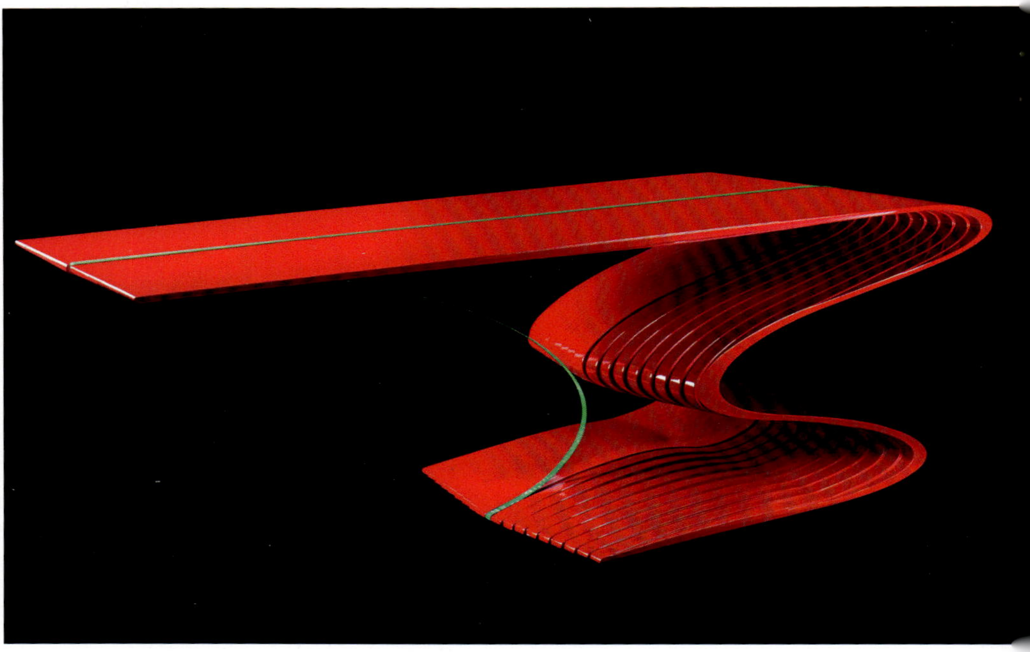

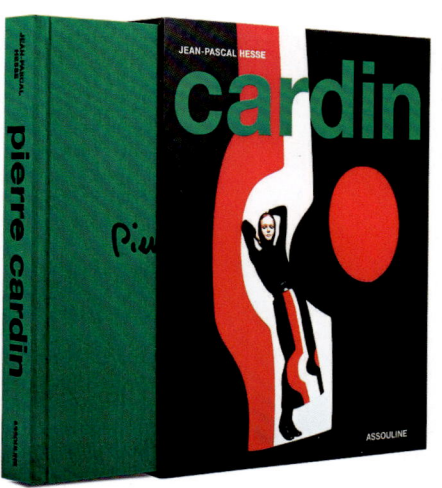

The first couturier to transform his name into a global brand, visionary French fashion designer Pierre Cardin celebrates 70 years of innovation. His unique creations testify to his fierce appetite for experimentation: His varied and ambitious creative universe encompasses fashion, accessories, jewelry, fragrance, furniture, fine restaurants, and an annual arts festival. Filled with fascinating images from the 1950s to today, this comprehensive anthology is the first to showcase Cardin's complete design vision, and portrays his daily life as a still-constant quest for new creative expression.
Text by Jean-Pascal Hesse, foreword by Marisa Berenson
11 x 14 in – 28 x 35 cm | 260 pages | 200 illustrations hardcover in a luxury slipcase | ISBN: 9781614285555
$195 – €195 – £150 | also available in French

> "MY FAVORITE GARMENT IS THE ONE I INVENT FOR A LIFE THAT DOES NOT YET EXIST, THE WORLD OF TOMORROW."
>
> PIERRE CARDIN

"WE WORK NOT IN CENTIMETERS BUT IN MILLIMETERS."

JEAN-MICHEL FRANK

FEBRUARY 2018

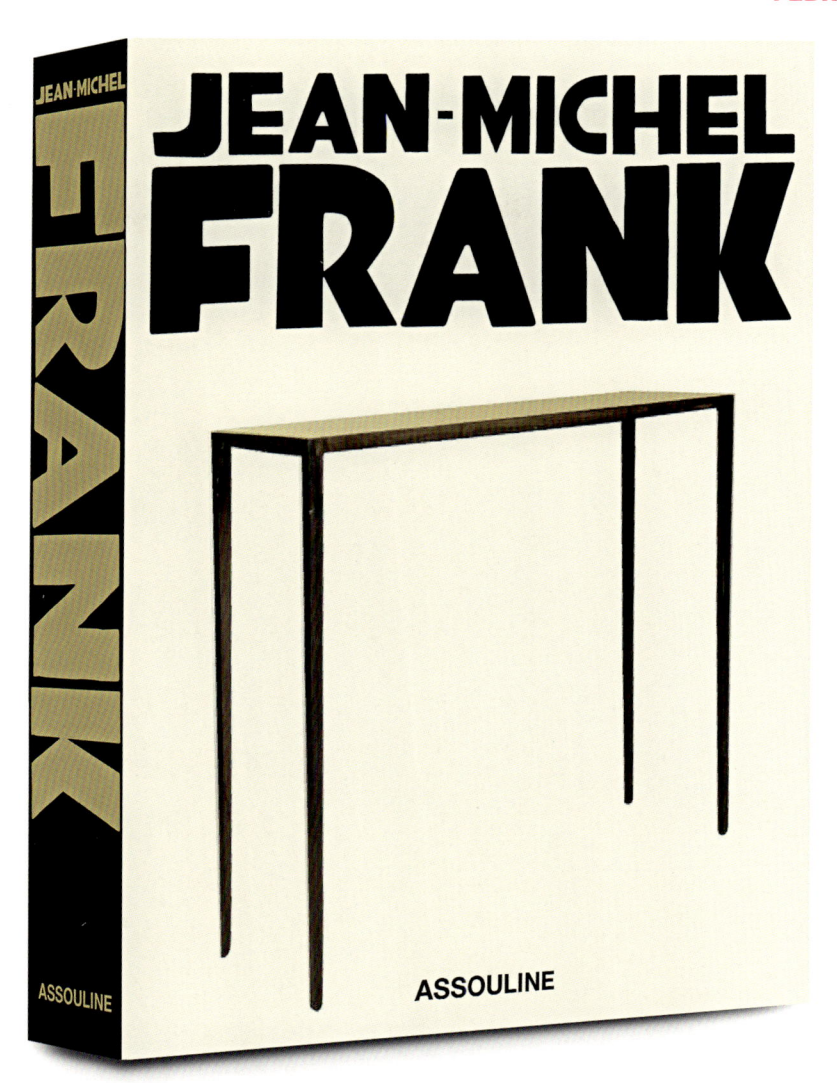

During the 1920s and 1930s, Jean-Michel Frank, the self-made man of interior design, honed and perfected his own unique style, which became a benchmark of Art Deco sophistication. Collaborating with the best artists, including Alberto Giacometti and Christian Bérard, Frank designed streamlined yet sumptuous furnishings and interiors for patrons such as Marie-Laure and Charles de Noailles, Nelson Rockefeller, and Elsa Schiaparelli. Just like the timeless little black dress, many of Frank's furniture designs still have the power to transform a space with understated elegance and continue to inspire. This definitive volume tells the story and shows the creations of one of the most influential designers of the twentieth century.

Text by Laure Verchère, introduction by Jared Goss | 12 x 15.5 in – 30 x 39 cm | 300 pages 300 illustrations | hardcover in a luxury slipcase | ISBN: 9781614285526 | $250 – €250 –£195

> "DIOR AND ASSOULINE PAY TRIBUTE TO ITS EMBLEMATIC ARTISTIC DIRECTORS BY DEDICATING EACH ONE A VOLUME, EXPLORING THE ESSENCE, INSPIRATION AND CREATIVITY OF EACH DESIGNER."
>
> ARTISALIVE.CO.UK

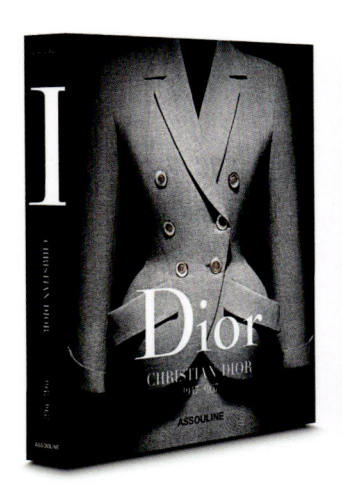

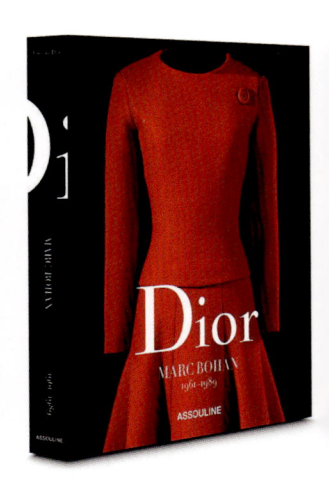

Christian Dior
1947–1957

NEW
Yves Saint Laurent
1958–1960

NEW
Marc Bohan
1961–1989

> "ILLUMINATES THE DIOR OEUVRE."
>
> ELLE

> "A BEAUTIFUL BOOK, RICHLY ILLUSTRATED WITH PHOTOGRAPHS HIGHLIGHTING ICONIC PIECES. A MUST-HAVE."
>
> VOGUE

Dior ★

Christian Dior	Yves Saint Laurent	Marc Bohan	Gianfranco Ferré	John Galliano	Raf Simons	Maria Chiuri
1947–1957	1958–1960	1961–1989	1989–1996	1997–2011	2012–2015	2016–

ASSOULINE

NEW

Dior
YVES SAINT LAURENT
1958–1960

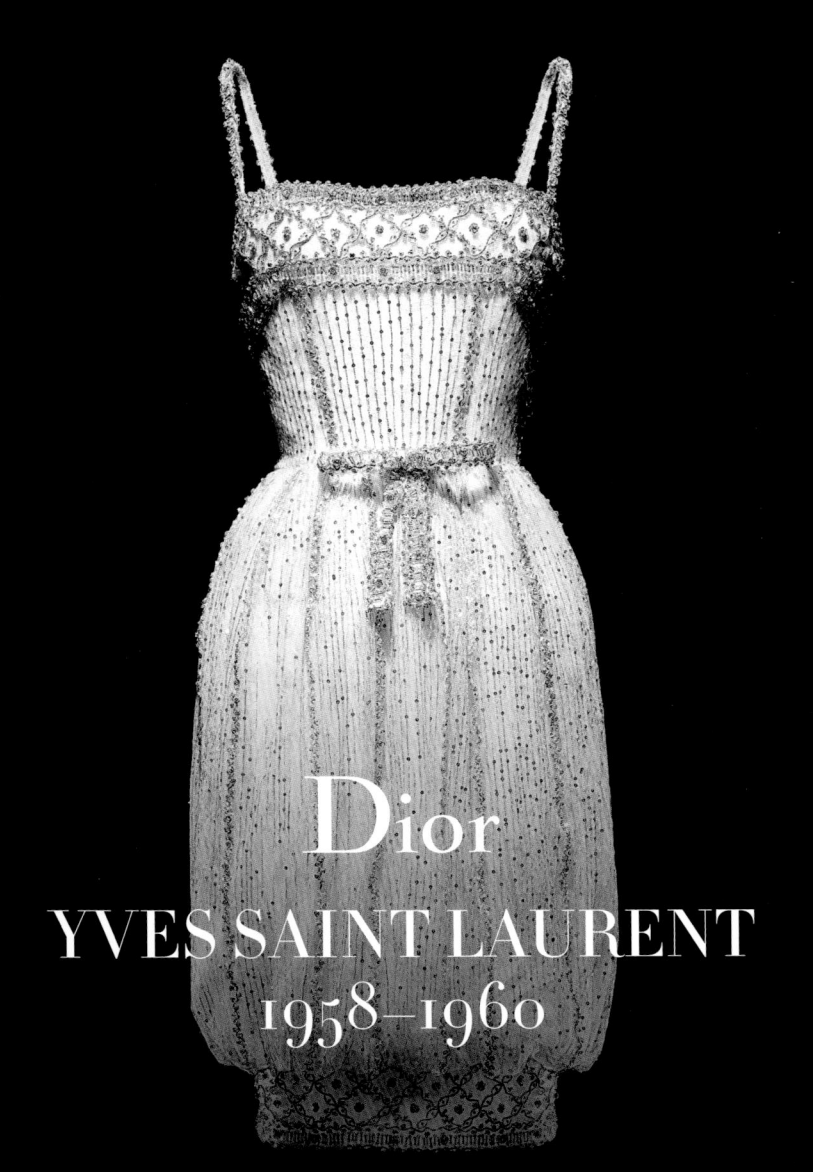

The second volume in this unprecedented series, *Dior by Yves Saint Laurent* showcases Saint Laurent's most iconic haute couture creations for Dior, from the Trapeze silhouette of his debut Spring-Summer 1958 collection to the beatnik inspiration for Fall-Winter 1960. Featuring beautiful photographs by Laziz Hamani and expressive text by Saint Laurent biographer Laurence Benaïm, this impressive volume provides profound insight into Saint Laurent's inspirations, influences, and vision for the evolution of the house of Dior.

Text by Laurence Benaïm, original photography by Laziz Hamani | 11.75 x 14.5 in – 30 x 37 cm | 300 pages 190 illustrations | hardcover with jacket | ISBN: 9781614285991 | $195 – €195 – £150 | also available in French

NEW

Dior
MARC BOHAN
1961–1989

The third volume, *Dior by Marc Bohan*, encompasses Bohan's most important haute couture creations for Dior, from 1961 to 1989, highlighting his understated elegance and soft, feminine silhouettes, beloved by socialites, celebrities, and royalty. Featuring beautiful photographs by Laziz Hamani and insightful text by fashion journalist Jérôme Hanover, including interviews with Bohan himself, this marvelous volume examines Bohan's inspirations and influences throughout three decades designing for the house of Dior.

Text by Jérôme Hanover, original photography by Laziz Hamani | 11.75 x 14.5 in – 30 x 37 cm | 400 pages 500 illustrations | hardcover with jacket | ISBN: 9781614286240 | $195 – €195 – £150 | also available in French

TOM VOLF
MARIA *by* CALLAS
In Her Own Words

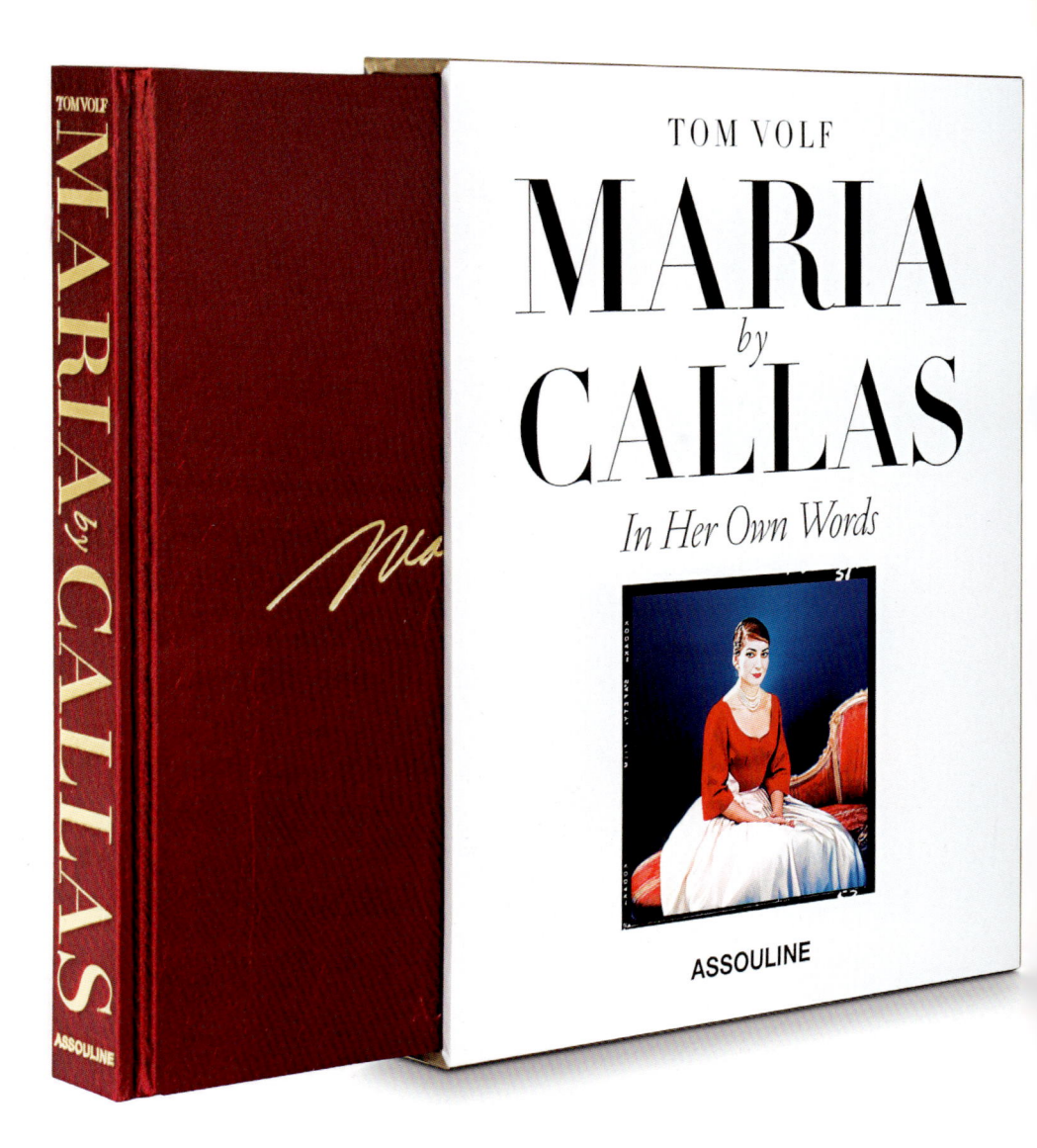

ASSOULINE

"THE GRANDEST BOOK EVER PUBLISHED ABOUT THE SOPRANO."

LE FIGARO

NEW

Decades after the legendary prima donna left the scene forever, filmmaker Tom Volf fell in love with Maria Callas. He traveled the globe to interview her closest friends and colleagues, who opened their collections, unveiling a trove of previously unknown photos, many of which came from Maria's own albums. Composed with the support of many of Maria's loved ones, including Nadia Stancioff, her longtime best friend, and Georges Prêtre, her favorite conductor, who for the first time in forty years agreed to collaborate on a book about her, *Maria by Callas: In Her Own Words*, the definitive, unique product of countless hours of research, offers a new perspective, a personal album as Maria herself would have presented, invoking the diva's own voice.

by Tom Volf, foreword by Georges Prêtre, introduction by Nadia Stancioff | 11 x 14 in - 28 x 35 cm 260 pages | 150 illustrations | ISBN: 9781614285502 | $195 - €195 - £150

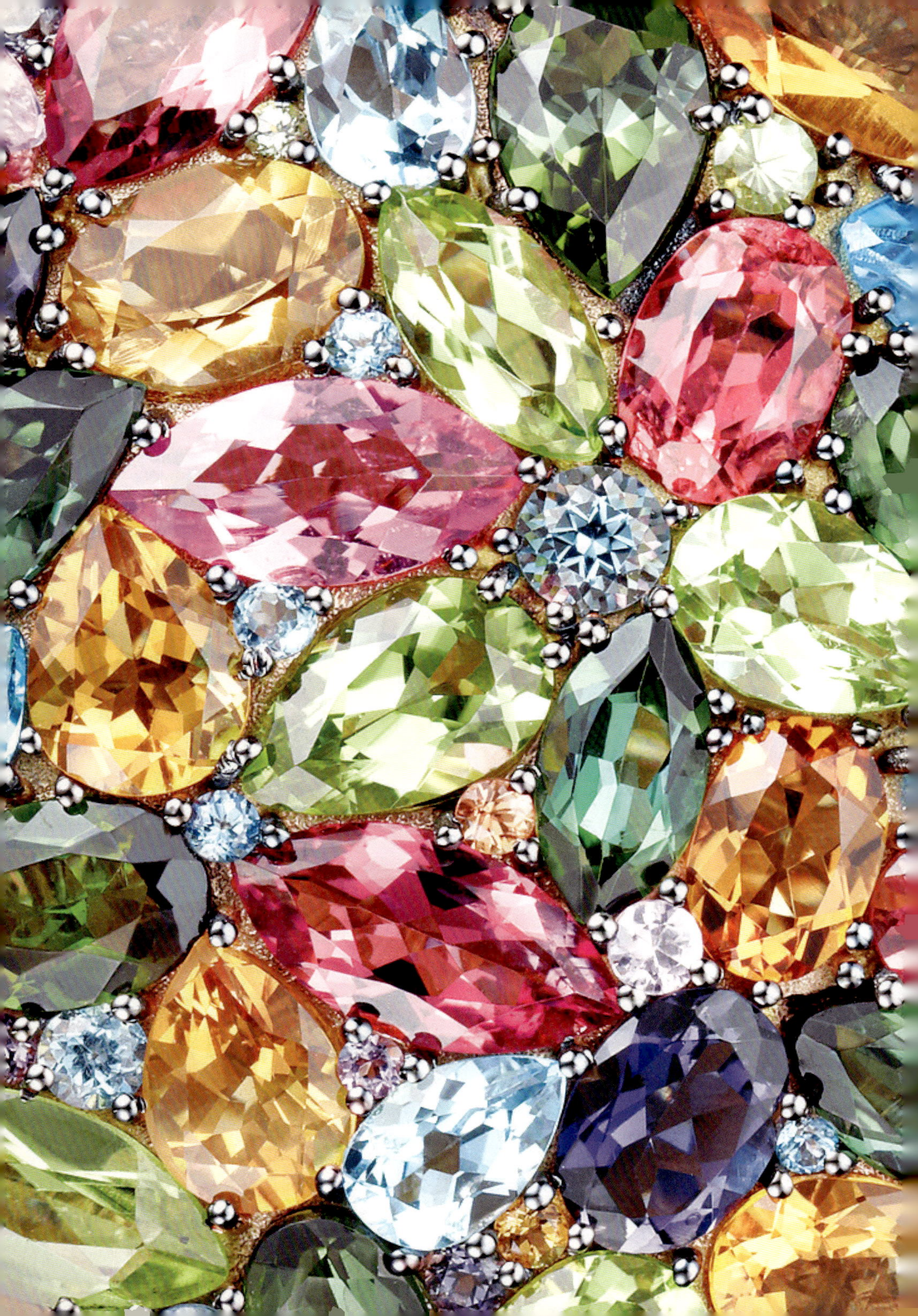

NEW

de GRISOGONO
GENEVE

DARING CREATIVITY

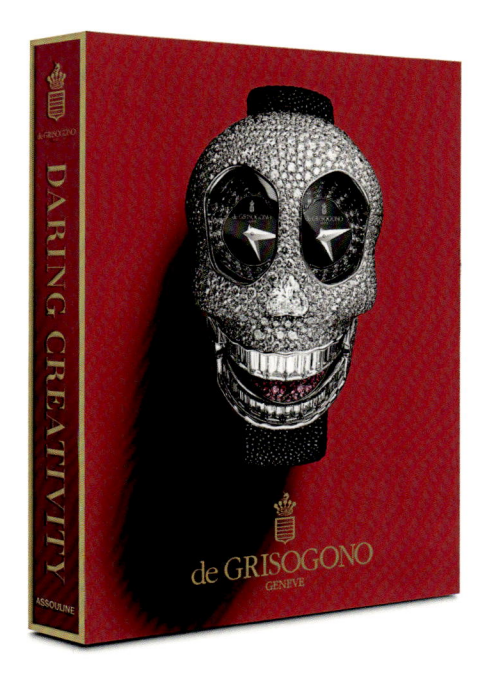

"I IMAGINE IN COLORS. I DESIGN IN LIGHT."

FAWAZ GRUOSI

Fawaz Gruosi, the inspired visionary behind Swiss jeweler de Grisogono, has been rejuvenating the conventions of jewelry since 1993. His glittering designs explore black and white diamonds, uniquely colored stones, and innovative yet classic forms. De Grisogono's opulent mix of Florentine and Byzantine influences, its striking gem combinations, and Gruosi's unsurpassed handcraftsmanship make the brand singular in the jewelry world.

Text by Vivienne Becker | 11 x 14 in – 28 x 35 cm | 256 pages | 160 illustrations | hardcover in a luxury slipcase | ISBN: 9781614285847 | $195 – €195 – £150

Allure Bookstand

DISPLAY YOUR FINE ASSOULINE VOLUMES ON THIS SLEEK AND ELEGANT BOOKSTAND, INSPIRED BY PIECES FROM THE FIFTEENTH CENTURY. A SCULPTURAL FEATURE TO ACCENTUATE ANY SOPHISTICATED ROOM OR CONTEMPORARY LIBRARY, THE ALLURE BOOKSTAND IS AVAILABLE IN A VARIETY OF WOODS, LACQUERS, AND FINISHES.

9.75 x 44.75 x 21.71 in – 101 x 114 x 53 cm | available in a variety of materials and finishes
ISBN: 9781614286455 | prices available upon request

> "I HAVE ALWAYS IMAGINED THAT PARADISE WILL BE A KIND OF LIBRARY."
>
> JORGE LUIS BORGES

NEW

CANADA GOOSE

GREATNESS IS OUT THERE

"WHEN YOU WEAR
ONE OF OUR PARKAS
YOU BECOME AN
URBAN ADVENTURER
YOU BECOME AN
ARCTIC EXPLORER
YOU CAN DEFY
ANY ELEMENT."

PAUL SILVERTOWN
CANADA GOOSE
VP, GENERAL MANAGER

A genre-defying brand at the forefront of its industry, an icon of adventure tested in the most extreme elements on Earth, delivering a highly stylish product while simultaneously remaining true to its roots, Canada Goose began in 1957 with functional, quality outerwear designed to protect police and military forces. Now, collaborations with celebrities and influencers have morphed the label into new areas of fashion, art, and design.

By Canada Goose | 11 x 14 in – 28 x 35 cm | 208 pages | 140 illustrations hardcover in a luxury slipcase | ISBN: 9781614286202 | $175 – €175 – £135

THE SPIRIT OF BENTLEY
Be extraordinary

NEW

Since its founding nearly a century ago, Bentley has become an arresting and eloquent voice for the British persona. This book not only illustrates the engineering excellence of the marque, but also introduces "today's Bentley Boys"—a tribe of Bentley and Britain adherents both inspired and motivated by what it means to be British. Featuring such varied creatives as Pink Floyd's Nick Mason, Alice Temperley, and interior designer Kelly Hoppen, this title is a celebration of the enlivening fire behind the brand as synonymous with the UK as the Union Jack.

Photography by Aline Coquelle and Laziz Hamani, text by Gelasio Gaetani d'Aragona Lovatelli
11 x 14 in – 28 x 35 cm | 300 pages | 250 illustrations | hardcover in a luxury slipcase | ISBN: 9781614285670
$195 – €195 – £150

FEBRUARY 2018

SEVAN BIÇAKÇI
TIME

"JUST AS THE ANCIENTS BELIEVE, JEWELS ARE MAGICAL, PERSONAL, PRECIOUS OBJECTS DEEPLY IMBUED WITH MEANING, WITH THE NOBILITY OF THE GOLDSMITH'S ART."

Sevan Biçakçi is a jeweler fit for an Ottoman emperor, bringing a mastery of traditional techniques largely unseen in contemporary metalsmithing and gem-cutting. An Istanbul native, Biçakçi is a visionary, fusing elements of Byzantine and Ottoman history, imagery, and architecture into his award-winning creations. Now, his designs have found an exciting new home in timepieces.

Text by Vivienne Becker | original photography by Kemal Olça | 11 x 14 in - 28 x 35 cm | 300 pages 150 illustrations | hardcover with jacket | ISBN: 9781614286332 | $195 - €195 - £150

Library Candles

Each candle: 3.5 x 3.5 x 3.5 in – 8 x 8 x 8 cm $50 – €50 – £38
Culture Lounge Candle ISBN: 9781614282853 | Havana Library Candle ISBN: 978161428284
Leather Library Candle ISBN: 9781614282839 | Paper Library Candle ISBN: 9781614282815
Wood Library Candle ISBN: 9781614282822

Classics Collection

THE CLASSICS COLLECTION IS ASSOULINE'S VIBRANT AND SPIRITED TREASURY OF DESIGN, ART, TRAVEL, CULTURE, AND FASHION. EACH VOLUME IS AN INSPIRING JOURNEY TO AESTHETIC BLISS, A UNIQUE WORLD ALL ITS OWN.

- CARLOS MOTA — *A Touch of Style*
- RENU KASHYAP, MAYA BOYD — **IBIZA BOHEMIA**
- AERIN LAUDER — **ASPEN STYLE**
- **DONALD**
- **THE BIG BOOK OF THE HAMPTONS**
- Condé Nast Traveller — **CHIC STAYS**

ASSOULINE

IT IS NO COINCIDENCE THAT DONALD ROBERTSON, KNOWN BY HIS INSTAGRAM MONIKER **@DRAWBERTSON** TO HIS ==HUNDREDS OF THOUSANDS OF FOLLOWERS,== HAS BECOME *THE FASHION WORLD'S FAVORITE ILLUSTRATOR.* HUMOROUS AND SHARP, DONALD'S WORK IS COLLECTED BY STARS SUCH AS **BEYONCÉ** AND FEATURED IN COLLABORATIONS WITH IT-BRANDS AND RETAILERS, EARNING ROBERTSON THE NICKNAME **"THE ANDY WARHOL OF INSTAGRAM."** FEATURING PLAYFUL ANECDOTES AND QUOTES FROM **INDUSTRY LEADERS, FASHION DESIGNERS,** AND THE ARTIST'S MANY COLLABORATORS AND MUSES, *DONALD IS ALREADY* ==*A COLLECTOR'S ITEM.*==

Foreword by John Demsey, interview with Donald Robertson | 10 x 13 in – 25 x 33 cm | 300 pages | 100 illustrations | hardcover with jacket | ISBN: 9781614286301 | $85 – €85 – £60

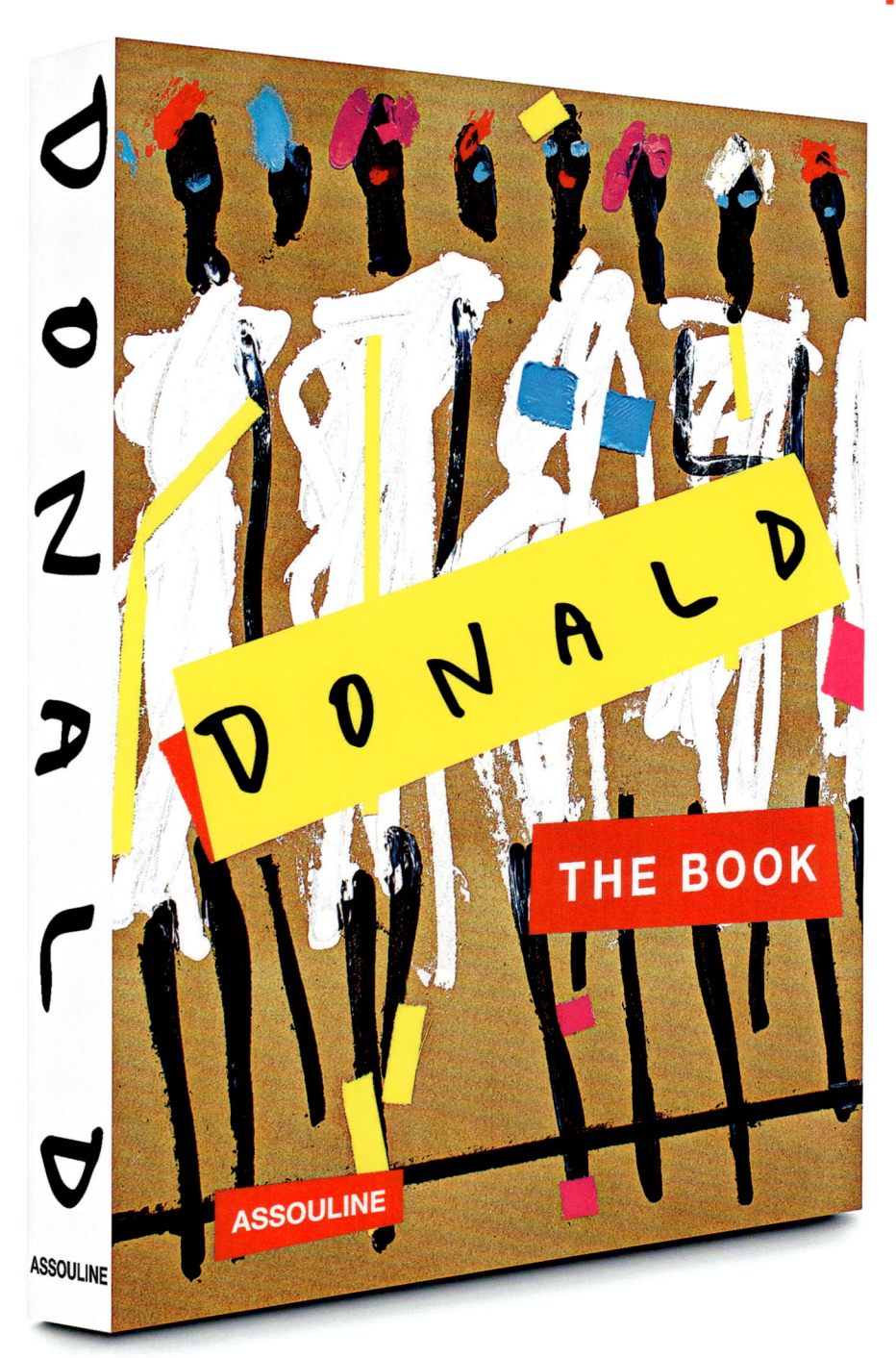

NEW

DONALD THE BOOK

ASSOULINE

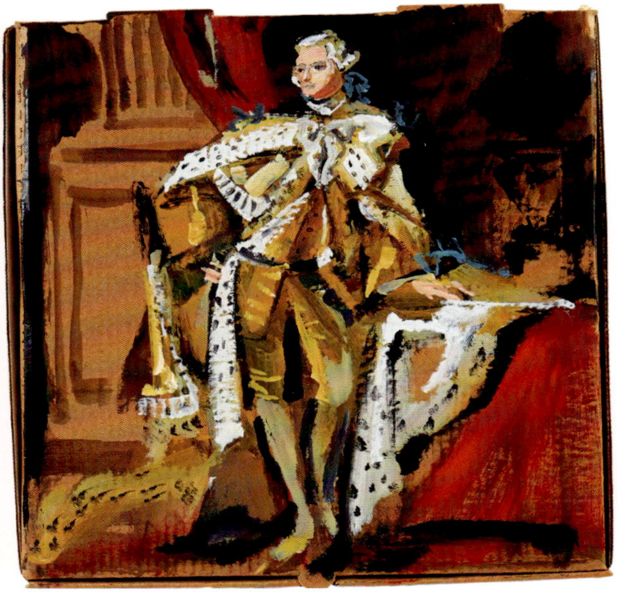

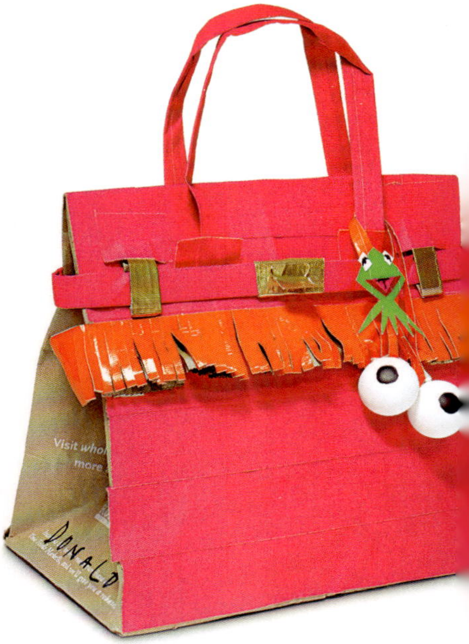
DONALD

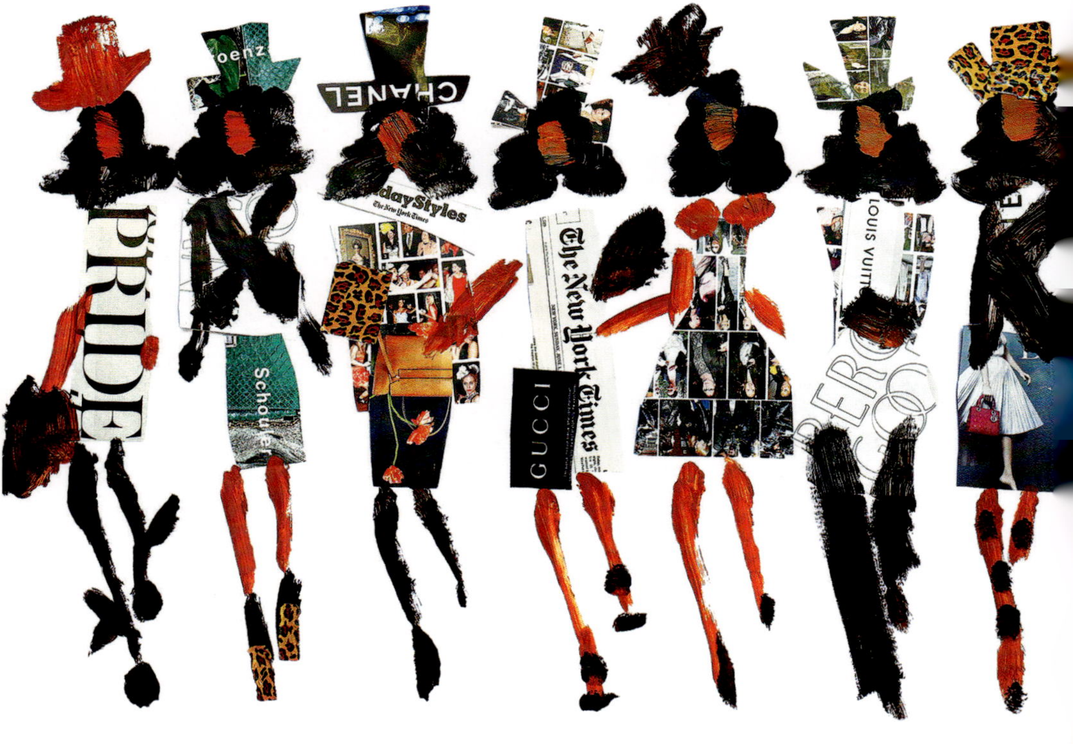
CHANEL
The New York Times
GUCCI
LOUIS VUITTON

> "I WOULD PREFER TO BE PAINTED BY DONALD ROBERTSON THAN ANYBODY ELSE. E'S THE DR. FEELGOOD OF THE ART WORLD."

LINDA FARGO

"DONALD ROBERTSON BELONGS TO THAT GREAT CATEGORY OF INSTANT ARTISTS. HE JUST GIVES A LOOK AT YOU AND CAN IMMEDIATELY DRAW YOU IN AN EXACT WAY, BODY LANGUAGE AND ALL!"

VALENTINO

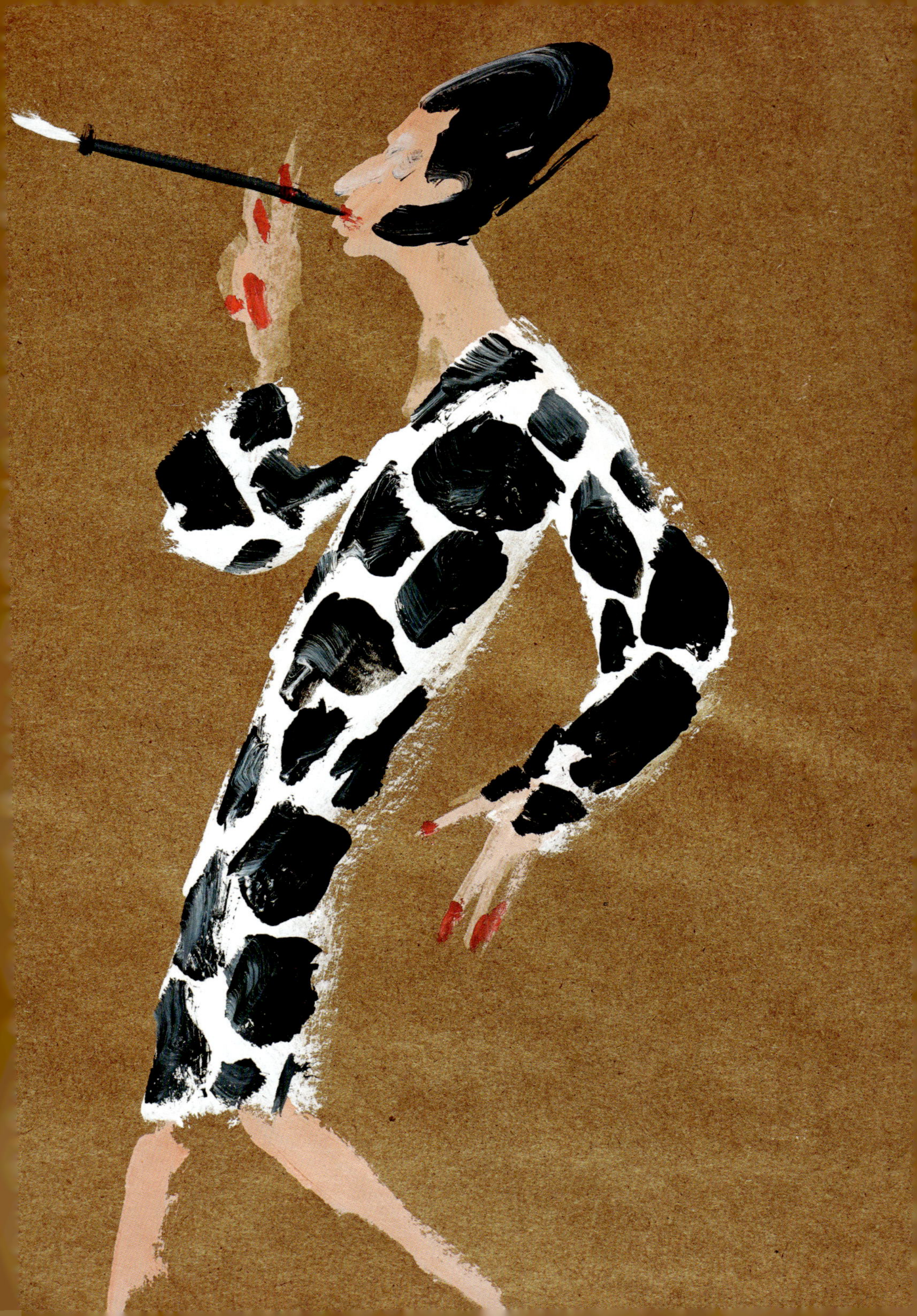

NEW

GUY BOURDIN
IMAGE MAKER

ASSOULINE

Protégé of Man Ray, principal photographer of *Vogue* France, inspiration for the fashion world's favorite photographers, and immortalized in the collections of museums around the world, Guy Bourdin irrevocably changed the face of modern photography. *Guy Bourdin Image Maker* is an exploration of the photographer's iconic imagery, featuring archival material yet unpublished, including original, never-before-seen *Vogue* layouts hand-clipped and annotated by the artist, Polaroids, and paintings.

Text by Matthias Harder, photography by Guy Bourdin | 10 x 13 in - 25 x 33 cm | 375 pages 200 illustrations | hardcover with tip-on image | ISBN: 9781614286356 | $150 - €150 - £110

"I AM NOT A DIRECTOR, MERELY AN AGENT OF CHANCE."

GUY BOURDIN

NEW

THE ARCTIC MELT
IMAGES OF A DISAPPEARING LANDSCAPE

> "DIANE TUFT'S STUNNING BOOK *THE ARCTIC MELT* COMBINES ART AND ENVIRONMENT TO CHRONICLE THE IMPACT OF CLIMATE CHANGE."
>
> MIKE BLOOMBERG

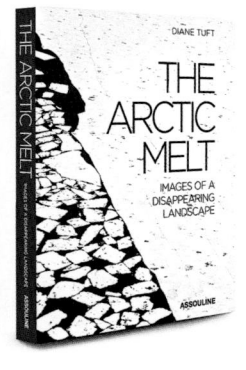

A brilliant new monograph by acclaimed photographer Diane Tuft, *The Arctic Melt: Images of a Disappearing Landscape* showcases her breathtaking and visually astounding journey to capture the ice in the Arctic Circle before the once-frozen landscape is rendered unrecognizable. Featuring stunning photographs of the icebergs of the North Pole, the mountain glaciers of Svalbard, Norway, and the ice sheet of Greenland, *The Arctic Melt* chronicles Tuft's passage through the waning tundra as millennia of ice thaws at a faster rate than ever before.

Preface, original photography, and haiku by Diane Tuft; foreword by Joe Romm
10 x 13 in – 25 x 33 cm | 176 pages | 80 illustrations | hardcover with jacket
ISBN: 9781614285861 | $95 – €95 – £70

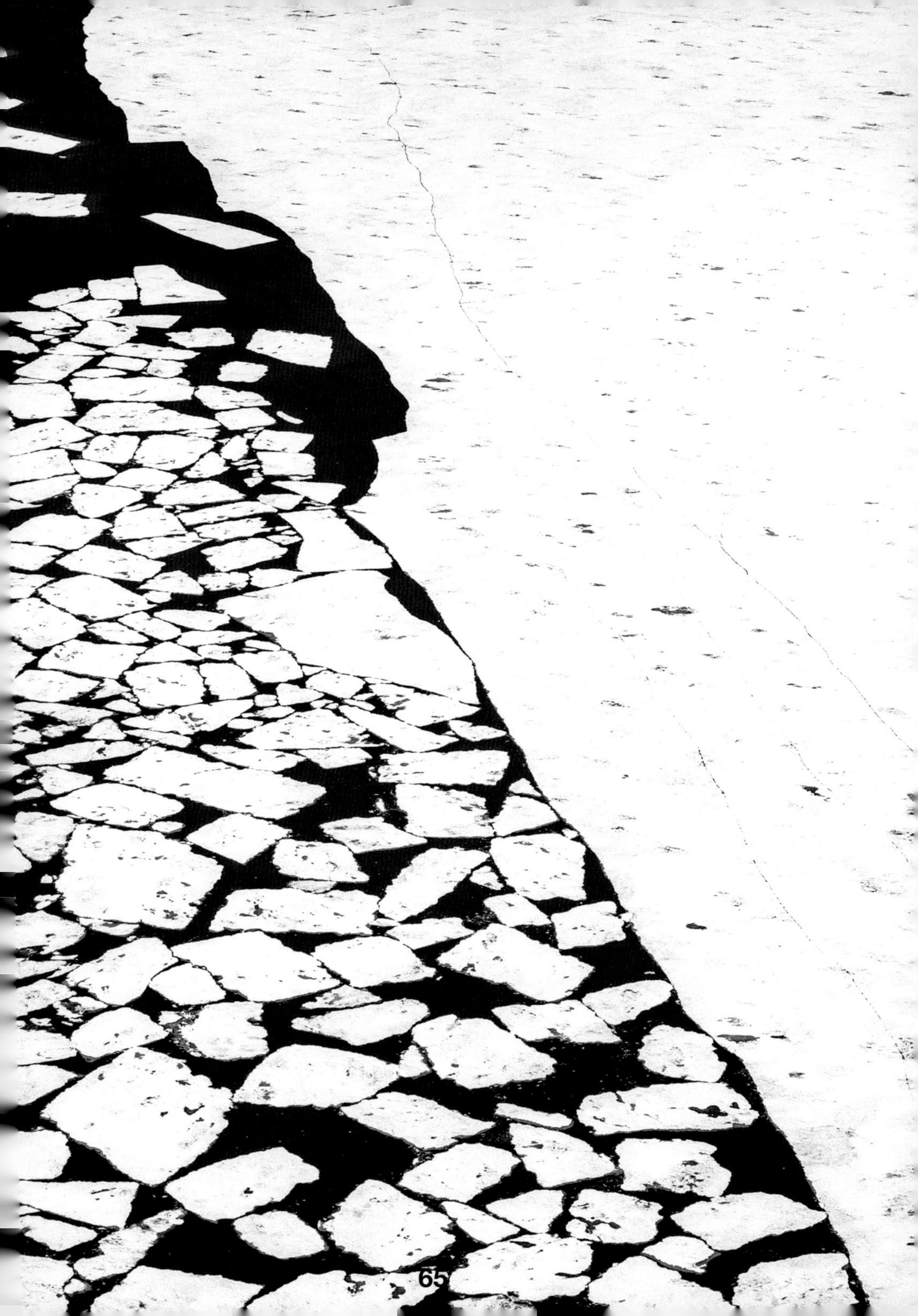

NEW

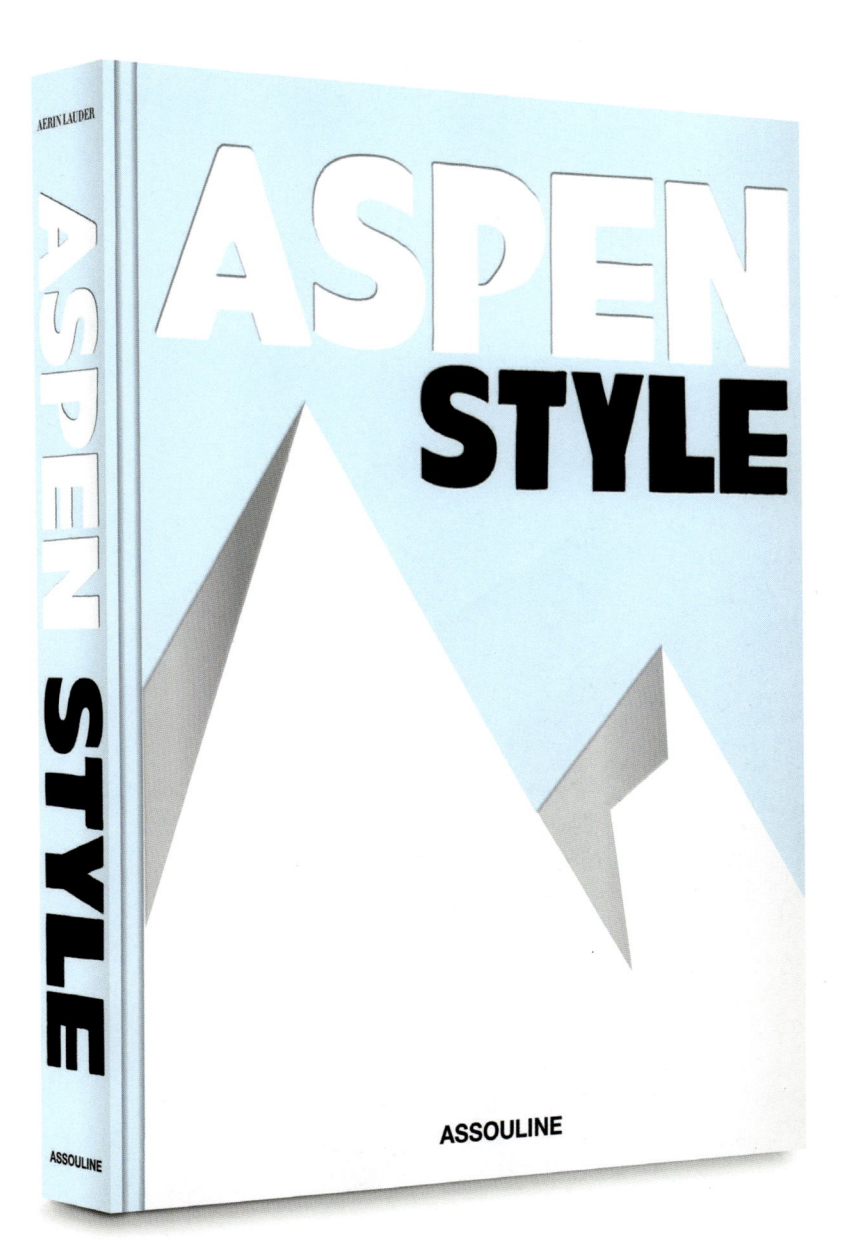

What began as a small mining camp in the late nineteenth century has become the preferred getaway of the world's elite. Aspen, Colorado, has a storied history almost as dense as the directory of A-listers who have adopted it as their second home. With an introduction from longtime resident Aerin Lauder, *Aspen Style* celebrates the stark glamour, working-class history, and romance of the virtually untouched landscape that gives the town its unique charisma.

Text by Aerin Lauder | 10 x 13 in - 25 x 33 cm | 270 pages | 160 illustrations | hardcover
ISBN: 9781614286226 | $85 - €85 - £60

"ASPEN IS MY WINTER PARADISE AND MY HAPPY PLACE. IT HAS ALWAYS BEEN, AND CONTINUES TO BE, MY SHANGRI-LA."

AERIN LAUDER

"THE COAST OF IBIZA IS ONE OF THE WORLD'S MOST MAGNETIC SPOTS. IBIZA BOHEMIA IS A BEAUTIFUL PORTRAIT OF THE ISLAND FROM SOME OF THE ARTISTS, HIPPIES, AND 24-HOUR PARTY PEOPLE WHO HAVE SETTLED HERE."

CONDÉ NAST TRAVELLER

From roaring nightlife to peaceful yoga retreats, Ibiza's hippie-chic atmosphere is its hallmark. This quintessential Mediterranean hot spot has served as an escape for artists, creatives, and musicians alike for decades. It is a place to reinvent oneself, to walk the fine line between civilization and wilderness, and to discover bliss. *Ibiza Bohemia* explores the island's scenic Balearic cliffs, its legendary cast of characters, and the archetypal interiors that define its signature style.

Produced by Renu Kashyap, text by Maya Boyd | 10 x 13 in – 25 x 33 cm | 300 pages | 200 illustrations hardcover | ISBN: 9781614285915 | $85 – €85 – £60

NEW

"*IBIZA BOHEMIA* IS A DELUXE, SHOCKING-PINK DIVE INTO THE MEDITERRANEAN'S STORIED PLAYGROUND."

THE NEW YORK TIMES

NEW

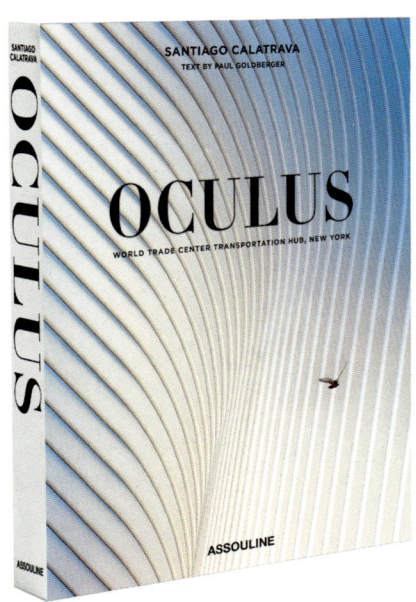

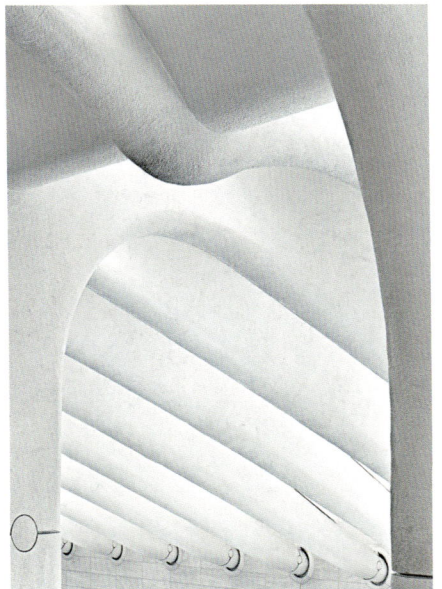

SANTIAGO CALATRAVA
OCULUS

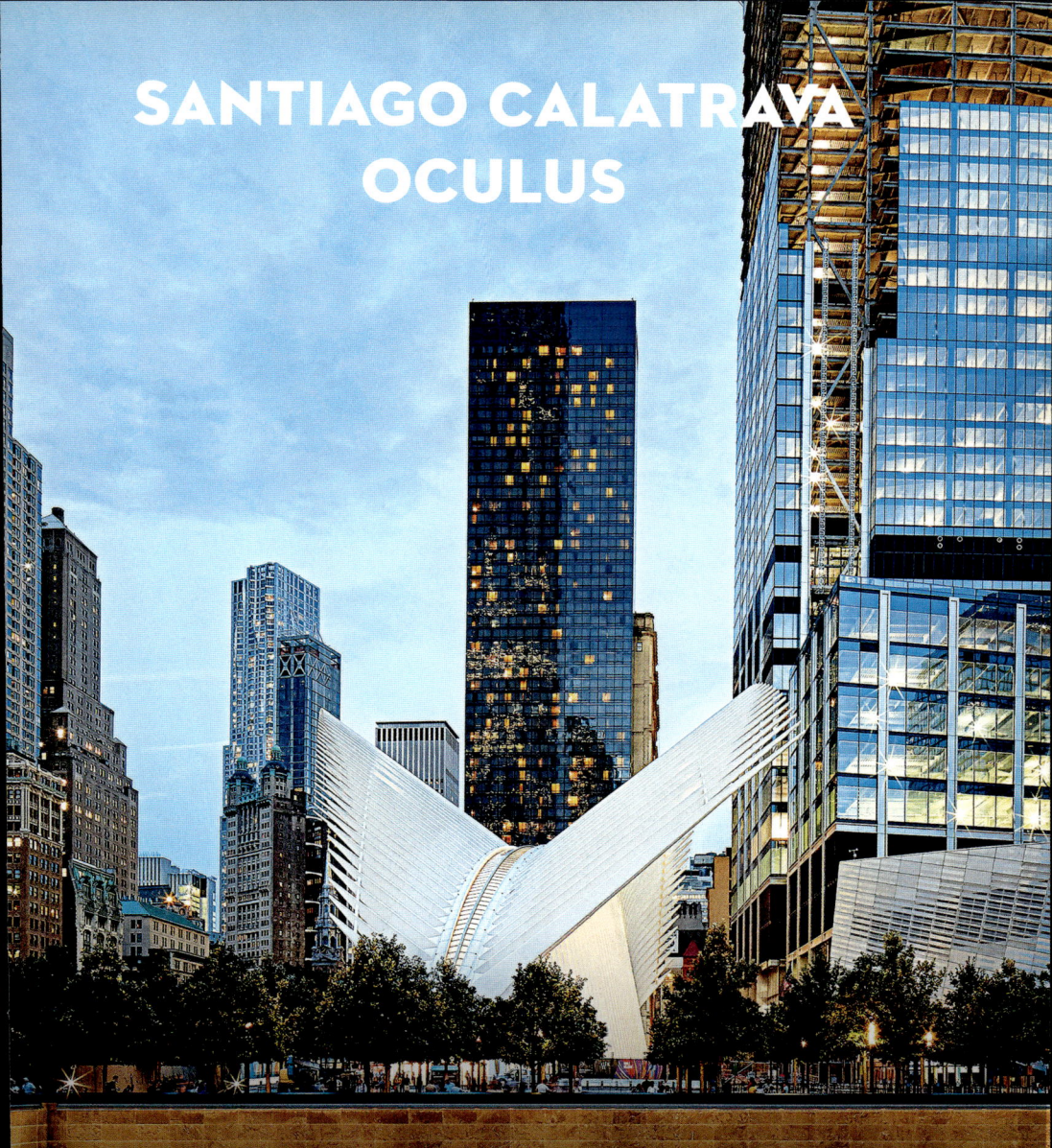

rchitect Santiago Calatrava is internationally renowned for the masterful conception and ngineering of public structures akin to high art. Taking inspiration from nature, his work imics the shapes and movement of organic entities, as witnessed in the recently completed Vorld Trade Center Transportation Hub in downtown Manhattan. *Santiago Calatrava Oculus* the authority on this already iconic structure, sure to be canonized as one of the most eautiful public buildings of the twenty-first century.

ext by Paul Goldberger, George Deodatis, and Santiago Calatrava | 10 x 13 in – 25 x 33 cm | 200 pages o illustrations | hardcover with jacket | ISBN: 9781614286295 | $85 – €85 – £60

72

FEBRUARY 2018

THE BOSPHORUS LIFE

As the crossroads of Turkey's European and Asian sections, the Bosphorus Strait is home to rich culture, incredible people, delicious food, unique architecture, and unmistakable style. Creative spirits have been awed and inspired here, and denizens and visitors alike are thrilled by the skyline, a breathtaking view of calming waters and magnificent bridges. But some of the best places to discover the style of the Bosphorus are within the private homes of its residents, which both pay homage to the country's glorious past and herald its future. *The Bosphorus Life*, showcasing 25 homes, is the melding of two continents, countless influences, and millennia of history.

Curated by Nevbahar Koç, original photography by Emre Guven | 10 x 13 in – 25 x 33 cm | 300 pages 150 illustrations | hardcover | ISBN: 9781614286516 $85 – €85 – £60

"A TRUE ARTIST IS NOT ONE WHO IS INSPIRED, BUT ONE WHO INSPIRES OTHERS."

SALVADOR DALÍ

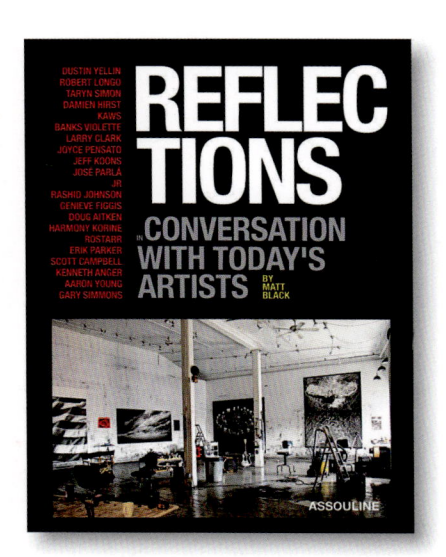

REFLECTIONS When filmmaker Matt Black interviews current artists, it's personal. His perceptive queries prompt these creatives to reveal intriguing pieces of their journeys. Jeff Koons explains the childhood experiences that made his art possible; Damien Hirst shares the motivation behind his spot paintings. These 21 conversations are casual, comfortable, and insightful. Illustrated with the artists' works, artists in their studios, and shots from Black's video interviews, *Reflections* is a unique foray from the printed page into the world of the cinematic, and a work of art in itself.
Curated by Matt Black | 10 x 13 in – 25 x 33 cm | 224 pages 100 illustrations | hardcover | ISBN: 9781614285359 $85 – €85 – £60

ART HOUSE Leading art collector Chara Schreyer's forty-year collaboration with interior designer Gary Hutton has produced five residences designed to house 600 works of art, including masterpieces by Marcel Duchamp, Andy Warhol, Donald Judd, Louise Nevelson, Diane Arbus, and Frank Stella. *Art House* takes readers on a breathtaking visual tour of these stunning spaces, which range from an architectural tour de force to a high-rise "gallery as home." An exploration of a life devoted to living with art and to designing homes that honor it, this title is an inspiration for art and design lovers alike.
Text by Alisa Carroll, foreword by Neal Benezra, photography by Matthew Millman | 10 x 13 in – 25 x 33 cm 224 pages | 150 illustrations | hardcover with jacket ISBN: 9781614285366 | $85 – €85 – £60

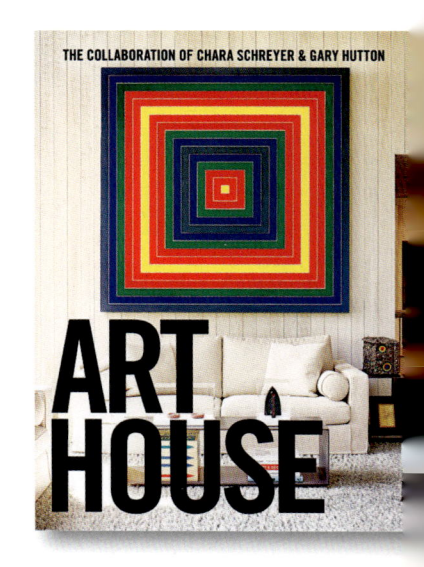

GIACOBETTI

NEW

> "WORKING WITH MODELS IS LIKE FLOWER ARRANGING. THE PHOTOGRAPHER TURNS THEM AROUND A BIT AND REARRANGES THEM, AND BEFORE YOU KNOW IT THEY'VE BECOME SOME NEW BEAUTY."
> — FRANCIS GIACOBETTI

Projecting fantasy and desire back into the genre of the nude photograph, into some of the most famed years of the Pirelli calendar, and into the portraiture of the world's most famous artists, actors, and models, Francis Giacobetti has created some of photography's quintessential images of the last half-century. Famous for blurring the lines between photography and painting, craft and art, Giacobetti's series—Zebras, Irises, Hymn, the Bacon portraits—have distilled the beauty of the human form.

Text by Jérôme Neutres | 10 x 13 in - 25 x 33 cm | 305 pages | 200 illustrations | hardcover with jacket
ISBN: 978161428615 | $85 – €85 – £60 | English and French bilingual edition

NEW

Beaumarly
PARIS

> "THE BEAUMARLY WAY OF LIFE IS EXPRESSED IN THREE WORDS: RIGHT, BEAUTIFUL AND GOOD."
> — GILBERT COSTES

Created by Thierry and Gilbert Costes, Beaumarly properties are icons of the Parisian lifestyle, encompassing more than 20 ultra-stylish cafés, hotels, nightclubs, and restaurants dotted around the City of Light, including Café Marly, Hôtel Amour, Brasserie Thoumieux, and Club Matignon. Celebrated for their unique ambience and atmosphere, each distinctive venue is a collaboration with the hottest designers, such as Christian de Portzamparc and India Mahdavi, and acclaimed chefs including Thierry Burlot and Sylvestre Wahid, exemplifying a true Parisian *art de vivre*.

By Gilbert & Thierry Costes, under the editorial direction of Yan Céh, foreword by Frédéric Beigbeder | 9.75 x 12 in – 24 x 30.5 cm | 188 pages 230 illustrations | hardcover | ISBN: 9781614281665 | $85 – €85 – £60 also available in French

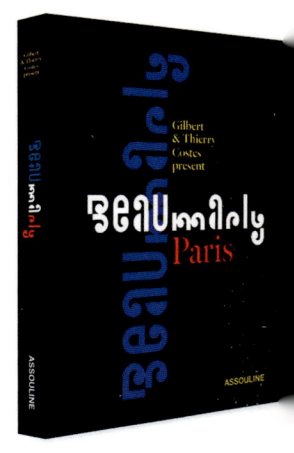

CHIC STAYS

CONDÉ NAST TRAVELLER'S FAVOURITE PEOPLE ON THEIR FAVOURITE PLACES

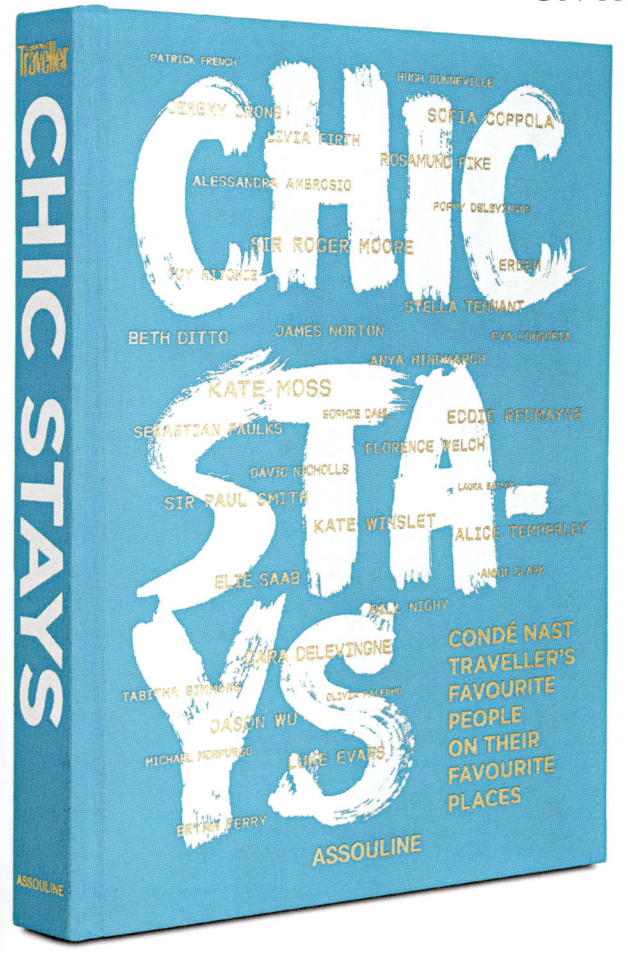

> "*CHIC STAYS* BRINGS TOGETHER THE WORLD'S MOST GLAMOROUS TRAVELERS."
> — THE TELEGRAPH

> "FOR THOSE LOOKING TO REALLY SKIP TOWN THIS HOLIDAY SEASON, SANS THE HEFTY AIRFARE, *CONDÉ NAST TRAVELLER* BRITAIN'S *CHIC STAYS* MAY SUFFICE."
> — THE NEW YORK TIMES

Take a tour of the world's most beautiful hotels with your favorite actors, writers, musicians, and models in *Chic Stays*. From Jeremy Irons's historical Palacio Belmonte escape in Lisbon, to the beaches of Kate Winslet's secret Scottish hideaway of Eilean Shona, to Kate Moss's favorite beach in the Maldives, each of these 36 personal tales of the loveliest spots around the globe is packed with anecdotes and lyrical descriptions to transport readers. The photography bursting across each page—from Parrot Cay to Sri Lanka to Oregon—inspires a new desire to discover these beloved corners of the world.

Curated by Melinda Stevens, edited by Fiona Kerr and Matthew Buck | 10 x 13 in - 25 x 33 cm
164 pages | 120 illustrations | hardcover | ISBN: 9781614285373 | $85 – €85 – £60

BEST SELLER

THE ITALIAN DREAM
WINE, HERITAGE, SOUL

"AFTER THREE YEARS OF CHASING ITALY'S MOST CELEBRATED WINES, FROM THE ALPS IN THE NORTH TO THE BEACH TOWNS OF THE SOUTH, INTERNATIONAL WINEMAKER COUNT GELASIO GAETANI D'ARAGONA LOVATELLI AND PARISIAN PHOTOGRAPHER ALINE COQUELLE CONSOLIDATE THEIR GRAPE-FUELED JOURNEY INTO A 366-PAGE LOVE LETTER—COMPLETE WITH LUSH PHOTOGRAPHY AND PASSIONATE MISSIVES—TO ALL THAT IS ITALY."

DEPARTURES.COM

"THIS IMMERSIVE, QUIRKY, AND QUIZZICAL TRAVELOGUE MAKES NO PRETENCE AT BEING A COMPREHENSIVE SURVEY, BUT IT DOES HAVE THAT ALL-IMPORTANT SOUL. DRINK IN ITS SUMPTUOUS PAGES ALONG WITH A DELICIOUS GLASS OF TAURASI. SALUTE."

VANITY FAIR

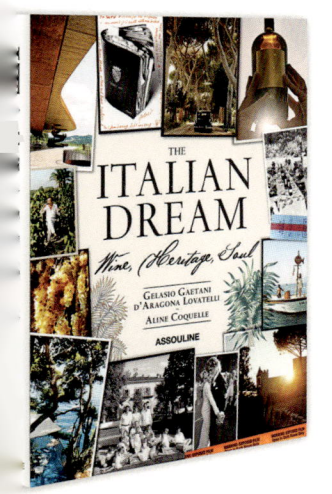

For more than three years, Aline Coquelle, the well-known globe-trotting photographer, and Count Gelasio Gaetani d'Aragona Lovatelli, a member of one of the oldest aristocratic Italian families, have followed the map of Italy's best wines. Guided by Gaetani, readers are introduced to a tribe of artistic and wine-loving *amici* who share their passion for their country's bounty. *The Italian Dream* is an escape into the effortlessly elegant Italian lifestyle, discovering hidden corners, savoring wine and sharing joyful times with convivial friends, from the foothills of the Alps to the hill towns of Tuscany to the relaxed southern seasides. Text by Gelasio Gaetani d'Aragona Lovatelli, photography by Aline Coquelle, foreword by Lapo Elkann | 10 x 13 in - 25 x 33 cm | 372 pages | 300 illustrations | hardcover with jacket ISBN: 9781614285199 | $85 – €85 – £60

ASSOULINE

The A Candle

The A Candle, Assouline's exclusive Culture Lounge fragrance candle in a luxury oversize apothecary-style ceramic holder, transports to a place of tranquillity with top notes of lemon and rum, vanilla-musk accord, and sandalwood base.

8 x 8 x 13 in – 20 x 20 x 33 cm
ISBN: 9781614285595 | $250 – €250 – £195

Maison Assouline, 196A Piccadilly, London.

NEW

ETERNALLY RITZ

The legendary Ritz on Paris's Place Vendôme is more than a luxury hotel; its very name evokes dreams of the City of Light. International luminaries from the worlds of high society, fashion, art, literature, cinema, finance, and diplomacy have illuminated its rooms, from the Duchess of Windsor, Gabrielle Chanel, and Ernest Hemingway to Maria Callas, Marc Chagall, and Marlene Dietrich. After four years of meticulous restoration, the Ritz Paris has again opened its doors, a glamorous star taking the stage with renewed spirit. This radiant volume overflows with elegant imagery illustrating the Ritz's esteemed guests and showcasing the impeccable work of architect Didier Beautemps and interior designer Thierry W. Despont.

Text by Laure Verchère, original photography by Robyn Lea | 9.5 x 12 in - 24 x 30 cm | 206 pages | 150 illustrations | hardcover with jacket | ISBN: 9781614285984 | $85 - €85 - £60 | also available in French

DINNER WITH JACKSON POLLOCK

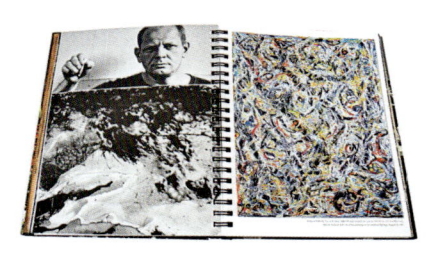

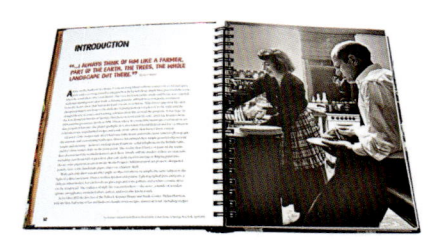

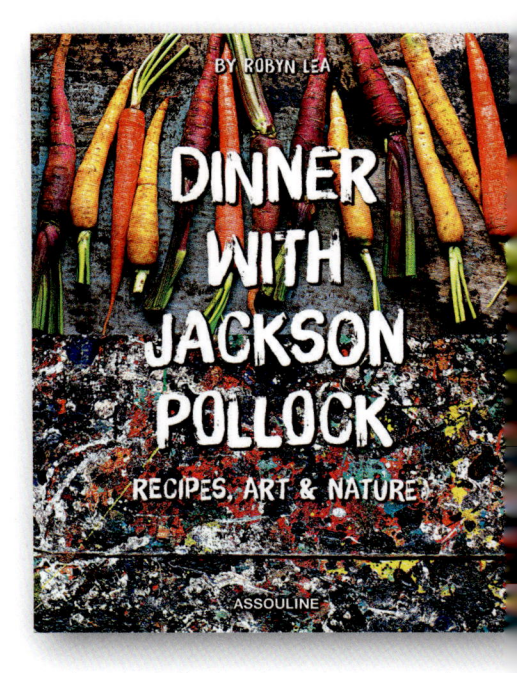

Jackson Pollock the artist needs no introduction, but lesser known is Pollock the gardener, baker, and party host. *Dinner with Jackson Pollock* features more than 50 recipes collected from handwritten pages by Jackson, his wife, artist Lee Krasner, his mother, or from their friends in the town of Springs on Long Island. Interspersed with Pollock's masterworks, still lifes of the Pollock-Krasner home, and delightful tales from the family and local friends, this is a unique and insightful portrait of a great American artist. Text and photographs by Robyn Lea, foreword by Francesca Pollock | 9.5 x 11.75 in – 23.5 30 cm | 176 pages | 100 illustrations | spiral-bound hardcover | ISBN: 9781614284321 | $50 – €50 – £3

DINNER WITH GEORGIA O'KEEFFE

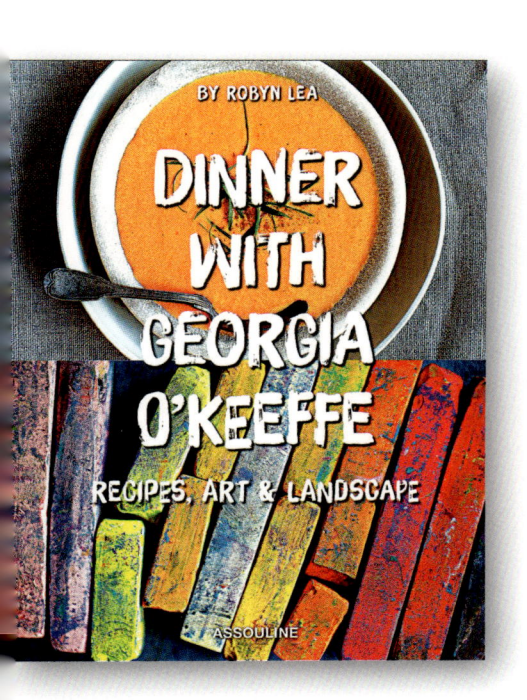

NEW

Georgia O'Keeffe chose New Mexico as the vibrant backdrop for her boundlessly creative life, refinishing her homes there with emphasis on the kitchen and garden spaces that were fundamental to her artistic process. Featuring [?]0 recipes collected from O'Keeffe's favorite cookbooks with her handwritten notes or prepared for her by cooks and caretakers, this book balances the fresh local and traditional ingredients she sought and the New Mexican landscape and culture that influenced her art and sense of self.

Text and photographs by Robyn Lea, foreword by Christine Taylor Patten | 9.5 x 11.75 in – 23.5 x [3]0 cm | 184 pages | 120 illustrations | spiral-bound hardcover | ISBN: 9781614285908 | $50 – €50 – £38

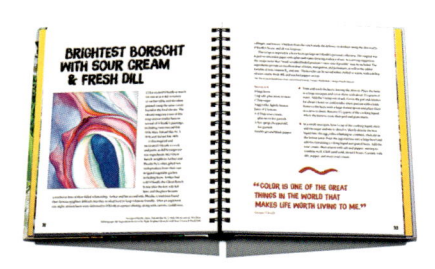

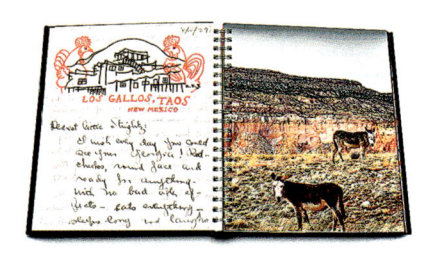

NEW

ALAIN ELKANN INTERVIEWS

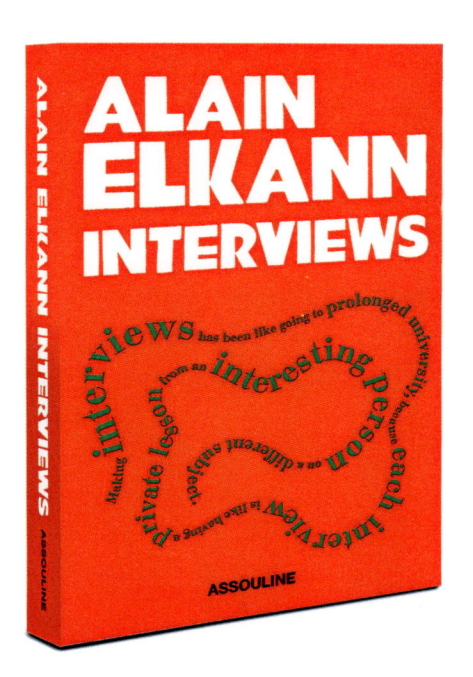

> "YOU HAVE TO BE EQUAL TO THE PERSON YOU INTERVIEW, EVEN THE MOST FAMOUS OR POWERFUL. THE INTERVIEW HAS TO BE LIKE A SHORT STORY: A BEGINNING, THE CENTRAL PART, AND THE END."
>
> ALAIN ELKANN

78 INTERVIEWS FROM 1989 TO 2017, INCLUDING:

BRIGITTE BARDOT, CALVIN KLEIN, DIANE VON FÜRSTENBERG, FRANÇOIS PINAULT, GIANNI VERSACE, HELMUT NEWTON, LUCIANO PAVAROTTI, MIUCCIA PRADA, SOPHIA LOREN, ZAHA HADID, SUZY MENKES

Alain Elkann has mastered the art of the interview. With a background in novels and journalism and having published over 20 books translated across ten languages, he infuses his interviews with innovation, allowing them to flow freely and organically. *Alain Elkann Interviews* will provide an unprecedented window into the minds of some of the most well-known and respected figures of the last 25 years.

Text by Alain Elkann | 6.25 x 9.25 in – 16 x 23.5 cm | 384 pages | ISBN: 9781614286387 | $35 – €35 – £2

"THE DETAILS ARE NOT THE DETAILS. THEY MAKE THE DESIGN."

CHARLES EAMES

NEW

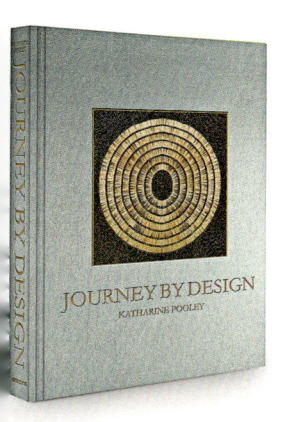

JOURNEY BY DESIGN British designer Katharine Pooley's refined, sumptuous interiors are inspired by a lifelong zest for adventure. Pooley has traveled extensively around the world, and her journeys are clearly reflected in her bold, eclectic, and daring designs. From the rustic country charm of Forter Castle in the Scottish Highlands, to a contemporary beach villa on the Palm Islands in Dubai, to the golden-red tones of a private residence in Doha, Qatar, Pooley's expert attention to detail shines in any setting. *Journey by Design* explores the creative process and diverse inspirations behind 19 of these inimitable spaces.
Foreword by Janet Jackson, text by Jennifer Goulding | 10 x 13 in - 25 x 33 cm | 264 pages | 400 illustrations | hardcover | ISBN: 9781614286288 $85 – €85 – £60

VENETIAN CHIC Venetian art connoisseur, interior designer, and hotelier Francesca Bortolotto Possati knows the intricacies of Venice. To have her as a guide is to experience firsthand her passion for the private side of the mythic city whose daily visitors outnumber its population. Join her to visit artists' studios, elegant Venetian friends, and palaces' secrets. Follow her on a gondola ride or through hidden gardens; discover restaurants, markets, and artisan shops. The discerning eye of photographer Robyn Lea makes this book a revelation of the Venice of dreams, which will surely allow readers to see this iconic destination through new eyes.
Text by Francesca Bortolotto Possati, foreword by Jeremy Irons, original photography by Robyn Lea | 10 x 13 in - 25 x 33 cm | 264 pages | 150 illustrations | hardcover | ISBN: 9781614285380 | $85 – €85 – £60

ASHFORD CASTLE Nestled on the shore of Lough Corrib, Ashford Castle has only grown in repute over the last eight centuries, passing through the hands of esteemed lords and ladies, hosting visitors over the years including King George V, Oscar Wilde, and John Lennon. The heralded estate even provided a setting for the Hollywood production of *The Quiet Man*, starring John Wayne. This publication will present the newly renovated Ashford Castle, a window into its illustrious past, and a preview of its promising future.
Text by Stanley Stewart | 9.75 x 12 in - 24 x 30 cm | 160 pages 100 illustrations | hardcover with jacket | ISBN: 9781614286172 $95 – €95 – £70

> "OF COURSE, THE O.G. IT GIRL WOULD HAVE A WHITE-HOT INSTAGRAM ACCOUNT (1.7M FOLLOWERS). STUDY HER PAINSTAKINGLY ART-DIRECTED POSTS— AND, YA KNOW, WORDS OF WISDOM— IN ASSOULINE'S DREAM NEW PINK TOME, *THE ART OF @BARBIESTYLE*."
>
> ELLE

This lively and charming volume showcases hundreds of beautifully detailed and accessorized lifestyle images from the @BarbieStyle Instagram page, vividly illustrating the modern identity and unique point of view of Barbie, following her fun and fashionable adventures around the world with her Girl Squad. Featuring inspiring texts written by Barbie herself, *The Art of @BarbieStyle* presents her affirmational outlook on life, travel, and the importance of celebrating special times with good friends.

By Barbie | 6 x 8.5 in - 15.5 x 21.5 cm | 280 pages | 300 illustrations | hardcover with tip-on image
ISBN: 9781614285809 | $50 - €50 - £38

NEW

"Barbie has been a contentious but indisputable style icon since 1959. But despite her age she's embraced social media. This new art book showcases the images created for the Barbie Instagram account—@barbiestyle has 1.7m followers and chronicles Barbie's fashion and travel adventures. That doll sure gets around."

THE OBSERVER

Icons Collection

THE ICONS COLLECTION IS A COLORFUL TRIBUTE TO THE GRAND ADVENTURE OF THE WELL-LIVED LIFE, FEATURING THE MOST EXOTIC AND GLAMOROUS DESTINATIONS AND FASCINATING CHARACTERS. THESE LAVISHLY ILLUSTRATED VOLUMES CAPTURE THE ESSENCE OF THEIR SUBJECTS. THIS COLLECTION FEATURES THE BEST-SELLING "IN THE SPIRIT OF" DESTINATION SERIES, LIFESTYLE TITLES AND INSPIRING MOVEMENTS SPANNING CENTURIES.

RIO
IN THE SPIRIT OF SEVILLE · ASSOULINE
IN THE SPIRIT OF ST. BARTHS · ASSOULINE
IN THE SPIRIT OF GSTAAD · ASSOULINE
IN THE SPIRIT OF CAPRI · ASSOULINE

NEW

THE LUXURY COLLECTION GLOBAL EPICUREAN

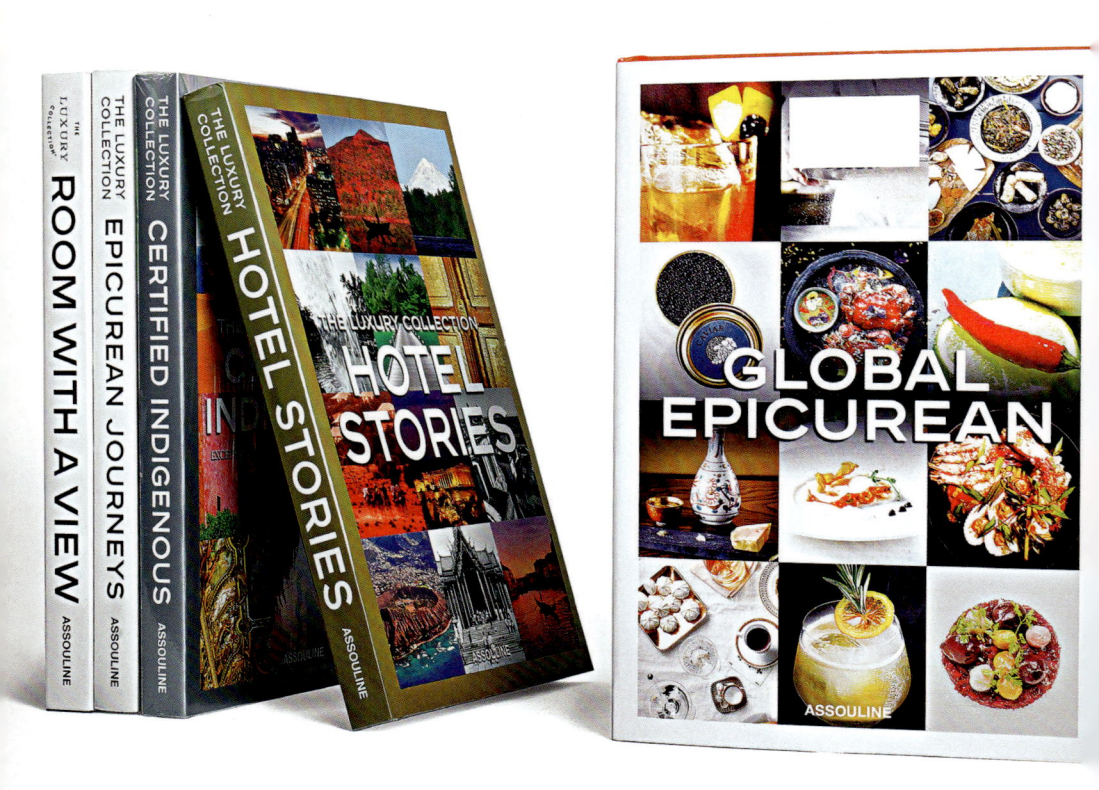

The fifth volume in The Luxury Collection series, *Global Epicurean* details exceptional gastronomic activities offered at these remarkable hotels, from private classes on Venetian cuisine with executive chef Daniele Turco at the Gritti Palace's epicurean school, to a Cretan feast at the Blue Palace, to private dune dining at Al Maha in Dubai. This book includes recipes from each Luxury Collection property that use ingredients native to the surrounding region. From starter to main course to dessert, local specialties take center stage, complemented by insights into local culinary scenes from noted cultural tastemakers and hotel chefs.

Introduction by Joshua David Stein | 7.5 x 11 in – 19.5 x 28 cm | 208 pages | 200 illustrations hardcover with jacket | ISBN: 9781614285922 | $50 – €50 – £38

Travels with Chufy

NEW

"SHE LOOKS AS COMFORTABLE ON THE ISLAND OF MAJORCA WEARING A HAND-PAINTED DRESS AS SHE DOES IN PARIS, WEARING COUTURE, IN THE FRONT ROW AT VALENTINO, OR ON HORSEBACK, GAUCHO-STYLE, ON THE PLAINS OF PATAGONIA (BUT SHE IS ARGENTINEAN, AFTER ALL)."

VOGUE UK

CONFIDENTIAL DESTINATIONS

Travel and style influencer Sofía Sanchez de Betak invites readers on a journey to off-the-radar hideaways where those in the know seek unforgettable experiences. Partake in the eclectic literary legacy of Naples's Albergo del Purgatorio, where guests are asked to leave behind a book of their choosing. Enjoy being surrounded by art at the Marco Polo Mansion, owned by a painter whose works in progress adorn the hotel. From the savannahs of Kenya to the glacial bays of Iceland to the soaring mountains of Patagonia, these vibrant stories will inspire travelers to explore beyond the known and experience the euphoria of cultural immersion and discovery.

By Sofía Sanchez de Betak | 7.5 x 11 in - 19.5 x 28 cm | 192 pages | 300 illustrations
hardcover with tip-on images | ISBN: 9781614285939 | $50 – €50 – £38

NEW

COCKTAIL CHAMELEON

**12 CLASSIC COCKTAILS,
12 UNIQUE VARIATIONS,
144 SIGNATURE COCKTAILS**

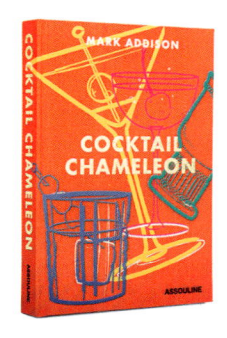

From the classic Margarita to the Love Byte, *Cocktail Chameleon* is award-winning designer and producer Mark Addison's invitation to join him as he dresses up 12 cocktails in 12 unique variations for 144 signature takes on the classics. Addison tantalizes with molecular mixology to create the Anti-Gravity, instructs on how to reinvent the beloved Bloody Mary with sake, and invokes the famed royal rose garden with the Versailles. Inspiring the creative mixologist in everyone, *Cocktail Chameleon* will become an instant ally for hosts looking to elevate an occasion, or a companion to help unwind and end the day on a high note!

By Mark Addison | 7.5 x 11 in – 19.5 x 28 cm | 240 pages | 144 illustrations | hardcover | **ISBN:** 9781614286196 | $50 – €50 – £38

NEW

TRANSFORM

60 MAKEUP LOOKS BY TONI MALT

Transform is a peek into the fantastic imagination of an editorial makeup artist. With a singl[e] model as her palette for these 60 stunning looks, Toni Malt works utter magic. While she detail[s] her inspiration and application process and reveals the encyclopedic product knowledg[e] that goes into creating each winning character, the spellbinding photos are the real proo[f] of her mastery of color, technique, and balance. Making use of such accessories as stencil[s,] Swarovski crystals, temporary tattoos, and glitter, Malt's looks range among soft and etherea[l,] impossibly chic, flamboyantly colorful, and truly otherworldly.

By Toni Malt | 7.5 x 11 in - 19.5 x 28 cm | 160 pages | 60 illustrations | hardcover with jacke[t]
ISBN: 9781614286608 | $50 - €48 - £38

NEW

COVA

Cova di Montenapoleone

Opened in 1817 by an officer who served under Napoleon, Pasticceria Cova quickly became the gathering place for Milanese upper crust and café society. Frequented by artists, musicians, intellectuals, and writers, not to mention the best place for midday coffee, Cova has remained a cherished fixture not only in Milan but globally as an integral patch in the fabric of Italy. On the occasion of Cova's 200-year anniversary, the *pasticceria* opens its doors to share its illustrious past, its glorious present, and its sterling future.

Foreword by Alain Elkann, text by Paola and Daniela Faccioli | 7.5 x 11 in – 19.5 x 28 cm | 184 pages | 100 illustrations | hardcover | ISBN: 9781614286615 | $50 – €50 – £38

Mémoire Collection

CHAUMET	A DISCERNING EYE
CHAUMET	AN ARTISTIC HEART
CHAUMET	CHAUMET EST UNE FÊTE

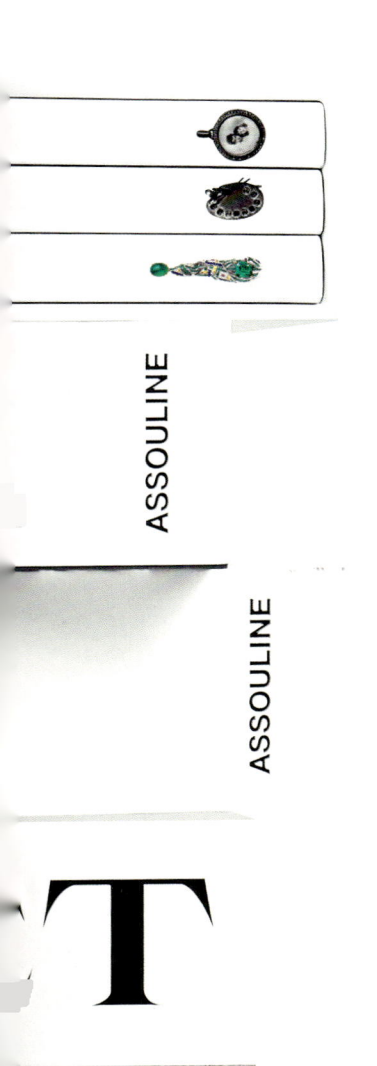

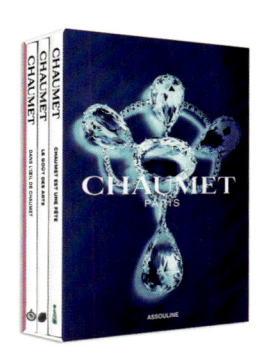

NEW

The fine jeweler Chaumet, established in 1780, is one of the crown jewels of Place Vendôme. This year Assouline introduces a second slipcase set of Mémoire volumes on the themes of Photography, the Arts, and Fetes, seen through the lens of more than two centuries of history and the evolution of Chaumet's artistic creations.
**Texts by Antoine de Baecque, Gabriel Bauret, and Jérôme Neutres
ISBN: 9781614286233**

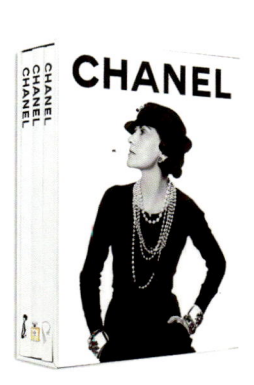

Self-inventor extraordinaire, Gabrielle Chanel revolutionized the lifestyle of her time by inventing a modern concept of luxury. Her vision thrives today thanks to the creative talents of Karl Lagerfeld, who has reinvigorated the house by reinventing its famous signatures season after season. This trilogy unfolds the spirit and heritage of the house of Chanel, from fashion to fine jewelry and perfume.
Texts by Natasha Fraser-Cavassoni, Vincent Meylan, and Martine Marcowith | ISBN: 9782843235184

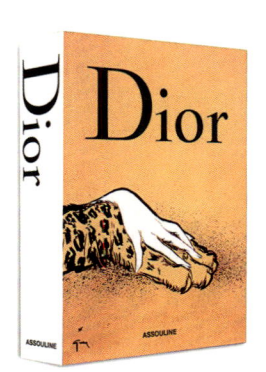

The pinnacle of French couture and savoir faire, the house of Dior is one of the world's most celebrated luxury brands. Presented in a collectible slipcase, these three elegant volumes capture the most enduring images from each decade of the brand's rich history, immortalizing Dior's couture, fine jewelry, and fragrances.
**Texts by Caroline Bongrand and Jérôme Hanover
ISBN: 9781614280200**

Each 3-book slipcase set:
6 x 8.5 in – 15.5 x 21 cm each volume | 80 pages each volume
approx. 60 illustrations each volume | hardcovers with jackets
$75 – €75 – £58 | also available in French

POKER

THE ULTIMATE BOOK

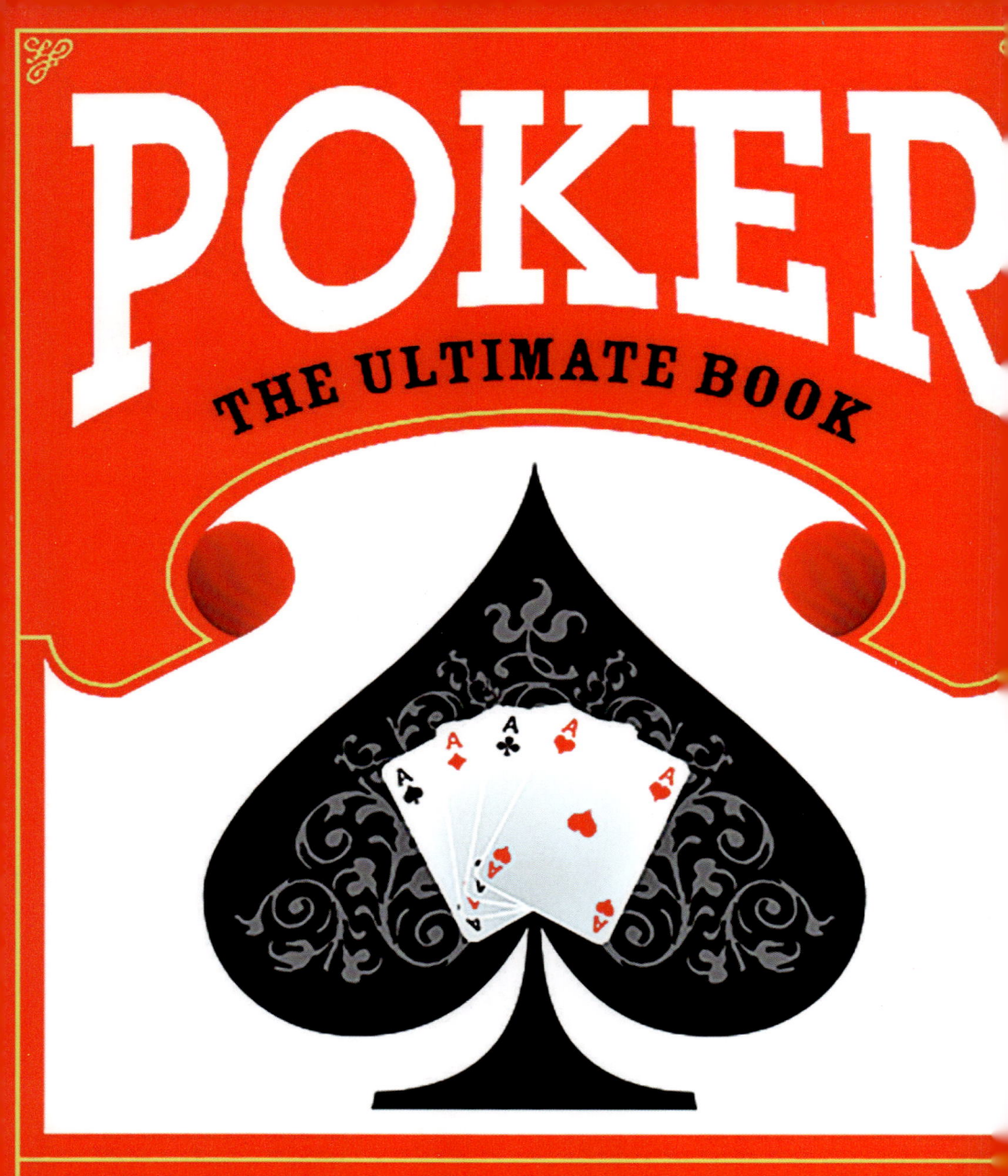

ALL YOU'VE EVER WANTED TO KNOW ABOUT THE MOST PRACTICED TABLE SPORT IN THE WORLD

HISTORY, LEGENDS, PSYCHOLOGY, CHEATING, MONEY, CASINOS, RULES, TOURNAMENTS, MOVIES, CHAMPIONS, INTERNET, DICTIONARY OF TERMS

ASSOULINE

"POKER TAKES FIVE MINUTES TO LEARN, BUT A LIFETIME TO MASTER."

MIKE SEXTON, PROFESSIONAL POKER PLAYER

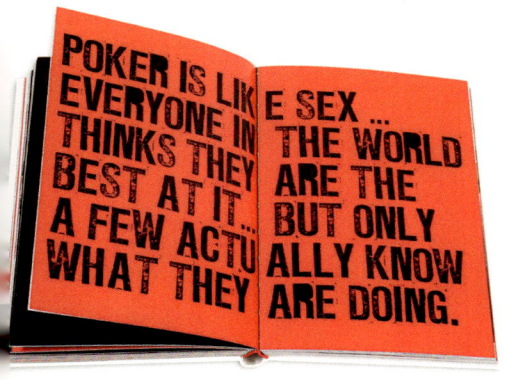

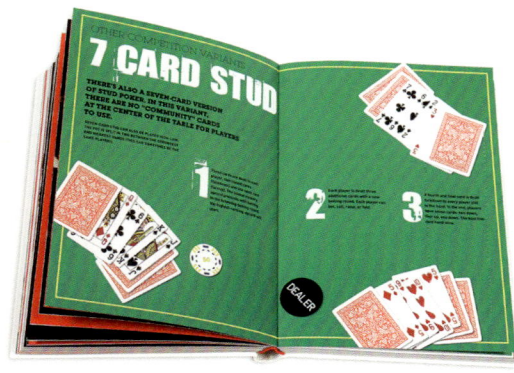

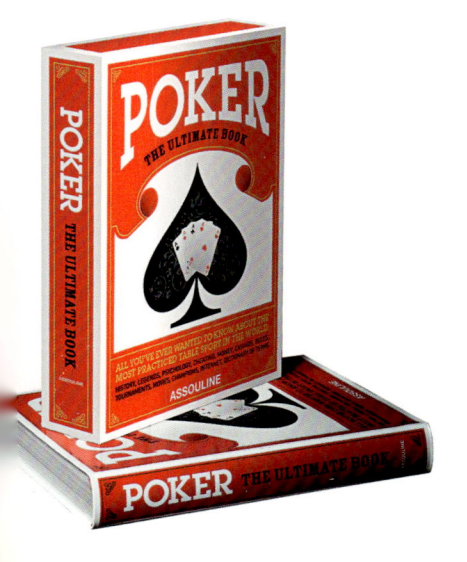

Poker: The Ultimate Book is a comprehensive guide to the most practiced table sport in the world and the perfect gift for the burgeoning player or the poker enthusiast looking to brush up on the game. The rules may be simple, but the practice itself entails a wide array of skills, all with millions of dollars at stake. This book invites readers to delve into the annals of the game, offering a narrative of its history and legendary players along with a detailed analysis of the basic rules, as well as astute tips that only an expert such as François Montmirel can provide.

Text by François Montmirel | 6 x 8.5 in – 15.5 x 21 cm
282 pages | 100 illustrations | softcover in a novelty box
ISBN: 9781614285533 | $50 – €50 – £38

TIM PALEN
THE HUNGER GAMES

NOMAD DELUXE
NOMAD DELUXE
NOMAD DELUXE
NOMAD DELUXE

THE SHOE
LIVING
RIO
CHANEL
MILLESIMES
Bordeaux

ITALIAN DREAM
LEGER

FOOD & LIFE
ASSOULINE

Cartier
Allure
LOUIS VUITTON WINDOWS
Louis Vuitton Windows
THE SUN COMPREHENDING GLASS AND
THE DEEP BLUE AIR T
LOVE FOREVER
THE ART OF FLYING
ASSOULINE
ASSOULINE

NEW RELEASES

FR ALSO AVAILABLE IN FRENCH

ANDY WARHOL
THE IMPOSSIBLE COLLECTION
ISBN: 9781614286271
$845 – €850 – £650

GOLF
THE IMPOSSIBLE COLLECTION
ISBN: 9781614286530
$945 – €950 – £750

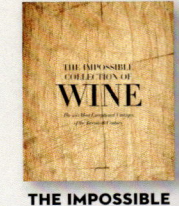

THE IMPOSSIBLE COLLECTION OF WINE
ISBN: 9781614284710
$845 – €850 – £650

THE HIDDEN COLLECTION
ISBN: 9781614286349
$845 – €850 – £650

BARBIE
ISBN: 9782759403110
$845 – €850 – £650

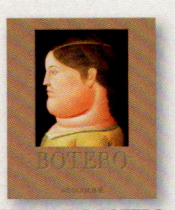

FERNANDO BOTERO
ISBN: 9781614284734
$845 – €850 – £650

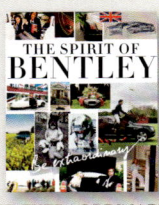

BE EXTRAORDINARY
THE SPIRIT OF BENTLEY
ISBN: 9781614285670
$195 – €195 – £150

BULGARI
THE JOY OF GEMS
ISBN: 9781614286158
$250 – €250 – £195

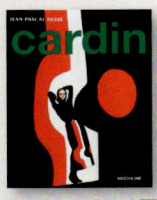

PIERRE CARDIN FR
ISBN: 9781614285557
$195 – €195 – £150

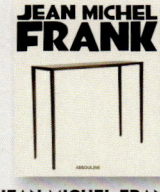

JEAN-MICHEL FRANK
ISBN: 9781614285526
$250 – €250 –£195

DIOR BY CHRISTIAN DIOR FR
ISBN: 9781614285489
$195 – €195 – £150

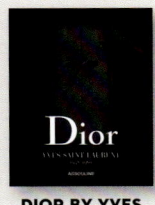

DIOR BY YVES SAINT LAURENT FR
ISBN: 9781614285991
$195 – €195 – £150

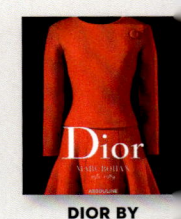

DIOR BY MARC BOHAN FR
ISBN: 9781614286240
$195 – €195 – £150

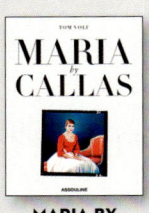

MARIA BY CALLAS
IN HER OWN WORDS
ISBN: 9781614285502
$195 – €195 – £150

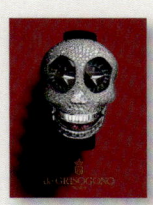

DE GRISOGONO
DARING CREATIVITY
ISBN: 9781614285847
$195 – €195 – £150

SEVAN BIÇAKÇI
TIME
ISBN: 9781614286332
$195 – €195 – £150

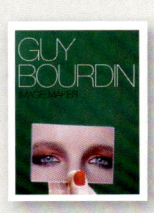

GUY BOURDIN
IMAGE MAKER
ISBN: 9781614286356
$150 – €150 – £110

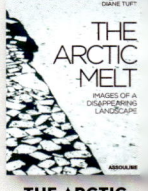

THE ARCTIC MELT
IMAGES OF A DISAPPEARING LANDSCAPE
ISBN: 9781614285861

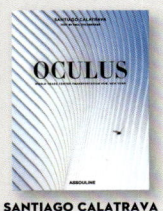

SANTIAGO CALATRAVA
OCULUS
ISBN: 9781614286295
$85 – €85 – £60

CANADA GOOSE
GREATNESS IS OUT THERE
ISBN: 9781614286202
$175 – €175 – £135

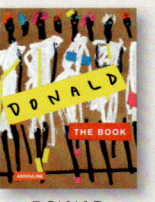

DONALD
ISBN: 9781614286301
$85 – €85 – £60

THE BOSPHORUS LIFE
ISBN: 9781614286516
$85 – €85 – £60

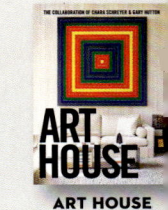

ART HOUSE
THE COLLABORATION OF CHARA SCHREYER & GARY HUTTON
ISBN: 9781614285366
$85 – €85 – £60

104

IBIZA BOHEMIA
ISBN: 9781614285915
$85 - €85 - £60

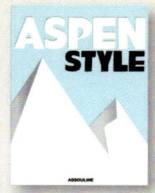

ASPEN STYLE
ISBN: 9781614286226
$85 - €85 - £60

GIACOBETTI FR
BN: 9781614286165
$85 - €85 - £60

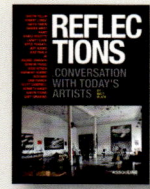

REFLECTIONS
IN CONVERSATION WITH TODAY'S ARTISTS
BY MATT BLACK
ISBN: 9781614285359
$85 - €85 - £60

THE ITALIAN DREAM
WINE, HERITAGE, SOUL
ISBN: 9781614285199
$85 - €85 - £60

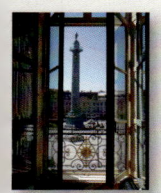

ETERNALLY RITZ FR
ISBN: 9781614285984
$85 - €85 - £60

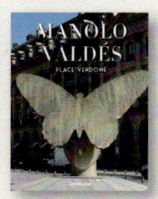

MANOLO VALDÉS
PLACE VENDÔME
ISBN: 9781614285960
$95 - €95 - £70

JOURNEY BY DESIGN
KATHARINE POOLEY
ISBN: 9781614286288
$85 - €85 - £60

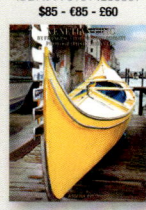

VENETIAN CHIC
ISBN: 9781614285380
$85 - €85 - £60

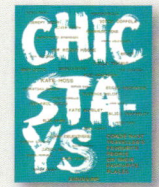

CHIC STAYS
CONDÉ NAST TRAVELLER'S FAVOURITE PEOPLE ON THEIR FAVOURITE PLACES
ISBN: 9781614285373
$85 - €85 - £60

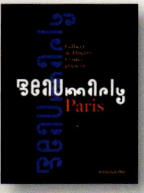

BEAUMARLY PARIS FR
ISBN: 9781614281665
$75 - €70 - £50

ASHFORD CASTLE
ISBN: 9781614286172
$95 - €95 - £70

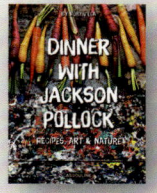

DINNER WITH JACKSON POLLOCK
RECIPES, ART & NATURE
ISBN: 9781614284321
$50 - €50 - £38

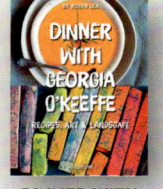

DINNER WITH GEORGIA O'KEEFFE
RECIPES, ART & LANDSCAPE
ISBN: 9781614285908
$50 - €50 - £38

COVA
ISBN: 9781614286615
$50 - €50 - £38

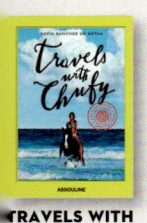

TRAVELS WITH CHUFY
ISBN: 9781614285939
$50 - €50 - £38

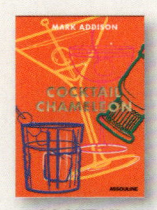

COCKTAIL CHAMELEON
ISBN: 9781614286196
$50 - €50 - £38

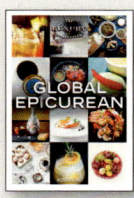

THE LUXURY COLLECTION GLOBAL EPICUREAN
ISBN: 9781614285922
$50 - €50 - £38

TRANSFORM
60 MAKEUP LOOKS BY TONI MALT
ISBN: 9781614286608
$50 - €50 - £38

THE ART OF @BARBIESTYLE
ISBN: 9781614285809
$50 - €50 - £38

POKER
THE ULTIMATE BOOK
ISBN: 9781614285533
$50 - €50 - £38

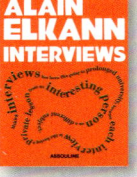

ALAIN ELKANN INTERVIEWS
ISBN: 9781614286325
$35 - €35 - £28

CHAUMET FR
PHOTOGRAPHY, ARTS, FÊTES
3-BOOK SLIPCASE SET
ISBN: 9781614286233
$75 - €75 - £58

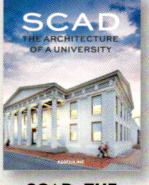

SCAD: THE ARCHITECTURE OF A UNIVERSITY
ISBN: 9781614285403
$85 – €80 – £55

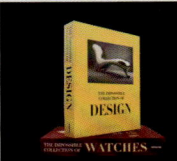

ULTIMATE COLLECTION
14 x 17 in
35.5 x 42 cm

NEW
ANDY WARHOL
THE IMPOSSIBLE COLLECTION
ISBN: 9781614286271
$845 - €850 - £650

NEW
GOLF
THE IMPOSSIBLE COLLECTION
ISBN: 9781614286530
$945 - €950 - £750

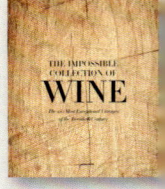

NEW
THE IMPOSSIBLE COLLECTION OF WINE
ISBN: 9781614284710
$845 - €850 - £650

NEW
THE HIDDEN COLLECTION
ISBN: 9781614286349
$845 - €850 - £650

NEW
BARBIE
ISBN: 9782759403110
$845 - €850 - £650

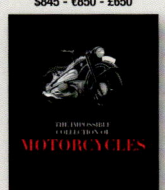

THE IMPOSSIBLE COLLECTION OF MOTORCYCLES
ISBN: 9781614280552
$845 - €850 - £650

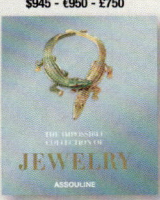

THE IMPOSSIBLE COLLECTION OF JEWELRY
ISBN: 9781614280583
$845 - €850 - £650

THE IMPOSSIBLE COLLECTION OF FASHION
ISBN: 9781614280163
$845 - €850 - £650

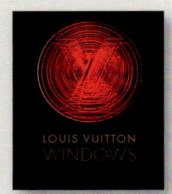

LOUIS VUITTON WINDOWS
ISBN: 9781614284505
$845 - €850 - £650

THE IMPOSSIBLE COLLECTION
ISBN: 9782759403004
$845 - €850 - £650

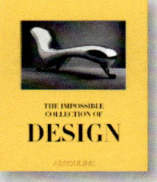

THE IMPOSSIBLE COLLECTION OF DESIGN
ISBN: 9781614282907
$845 - €850 - £650

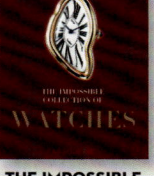

THE IMPOSSIBLE COLLECTION OF WATCHES
ISBN: 9781614282105
$845 - €850 - £650

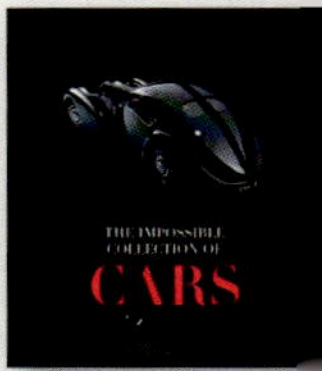

THE IMPOSSIBLE COLLECTION OF CARS
ISBN: 9781614280156
$845 - €850 - £650

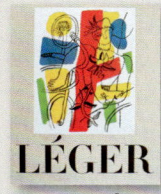

FERNAND LÉGER
A SURVEY OF ICONIC WORKS
ISBN: 9781614280057
$845 - €850 - £650

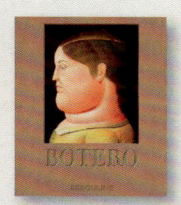

FERNANDO BOTERO
ISBN: 9781614284734
$845 - €850 - £650

SPECIAL EDITION 
FERNANDO BOTERO
SIGNED NUMBERED EDITION
ISBN: 9781614284772
$1,750 - €1,750 - £1,350

VENICE SYNAGOGUES
ISBN: 9781614280521
$845 - €850 - £650

SPECIAL EDITION 
VENICE SYNAGOGUES
SPECIAL EDITION
ISBN: 9781614282471
$4,500 - €4,500 - £3,500

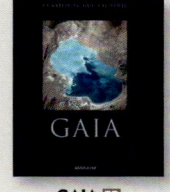

GAIA FR
ISBN: 9782759405336
$845 - €850 - £650

OSCAR NIEMEYER
ISBN: 9782759402939
$845 - €850 - £650

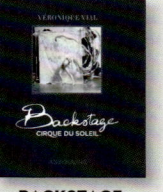

BACKSTAGE CIRQUE DU SOLEIL FR
ISBN: 9781614282983
$845 - €850 - £650

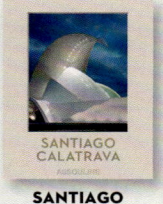

SANTIAGO CALATRAVA
ISBN: 9781614281443
$845 - €850 - £650

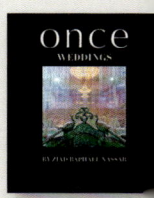

ONCE WEDDINGS
ISBN: 9781614280484
$845 - €850 - £650

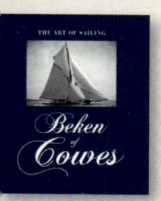

BEKEN OF COWES
THE ART OF SAILING
ISBN: 9781614280194
$845 - €850 - £650

THE QUEEN'S PEOPLE
ISBN: 9781614285298
$845 - €850 - £650

BALLETS RUSSES FR
ISBN: 9781614280149
$345 - €850 - £650

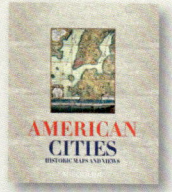

AMERICAN CITIES
ISBN: 9781614282891
$845 - €850 - £650

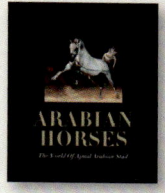

ARABIAN HORSES
THE WORLD OF AJMAL ARABIAN STUD
ISBN: 9781614280767
$845 - €850 - £650

HYUNDAI
LIVE BRILLIANT
ISBN: 9781614282310
$845 - €850 - £650

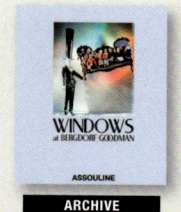

WINDOWS AT BERGDORF GOODMAN
ARCHIVE
ISBN: 9782759404759

VERUSCHKA
ARCHIVE
ISBN: 9782759402960

SPECIAL EDITIONS

RAJASTHAN STYLE
ISBN: 9781614284833
$695 - €695 - £525

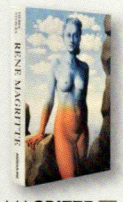

MAGRITTE FR
L'EMPIRE DES IMAGES
ISBN: 9782843235092
$250 - €250 - £195

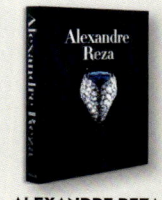

ALEXANDRE REZA
ISBN: 9782759404643
$845 - €850 - £650

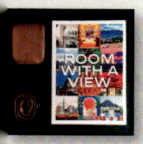

THE LUXURY COLLECTION
ROOM WITH A VIEW
ISBN: 9781614285564
$950 - €960 - £750

THE LUXURY COLLECTION
DESTINATION GUIDES
ISBN: 9782759404629
$150 - €150 - £110

THE LUXURY COLLECTION
EPICUREAN JOURNEYS
ISBN: 9781614282914
$150 - €150 - £110

HAGGADAH FR
ISBN: 9782843232510
$845 - €850 - £650

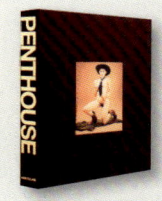

PENTHOUSE
SPECIAL EDITION
ISBN: 9782759402946
$845 - €850 - £650

SOUTH POLE
THE BRITISH ANTARCTIC EXPEDITION 1910-1913
WATERPROOF EDITION
LIMITED TO 150 COPIES
ISBN: 9781614280385
$4,500 - €4,500 - £3,500

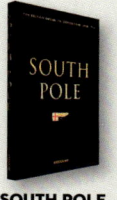

SOUTH POLE
THE BRITISH ANTARCTIC EXPEDITION 1910-1913
SPECIAL EDITION
ISBN: 9781614280118
$1,050 - €1,050 - £825

GAIA FR
SPECIAL EDITION
ISBN: 9782759405367
$7,000 - €7,075 - £5,250

PORTRAITS AND CAFTANS OF THE OTTOMAN SULTANS
ARCHIVE
ISBN: 9781614281108

LEGENDS COLLECTION
11 x 14 in
28 x 35 cm

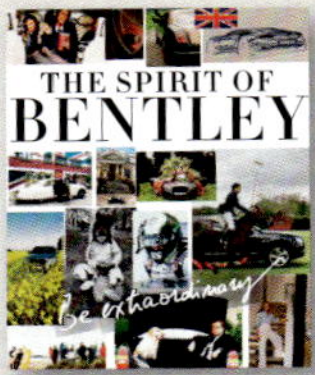

NEW
BE EXTRAORDINARY
THE SPIRIT OF BENTLEY
ISBN: 9781614285670
$195 – €195 – £150

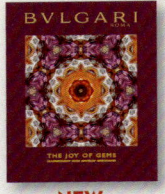

NEW
BULGARI
THE JOY OF GEMS MAGNIFICENT HIGH JEWELRY CREATIONS
ISBN: 9781614286158
$250 – €250 – £195

NEW
CANADA GOOSE
GREATNESS IS OUT THE
ISBN: 9781614286202
$175 – €175 – £135

NEW
DE GRISOGONO
DARING CREATIVITY
ISBN: 9781614285847
$195 – €195 – £150

NEW
JEAN-MICHEL FRANK
ISBN: 9781614285526
$250 – €250 –£195

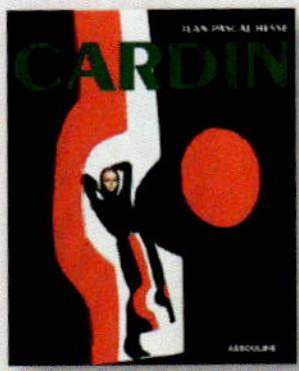

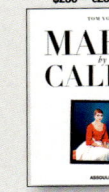

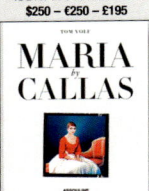

NEW
PIERRE CARDIN FR
ISBN: 9781614285557
$195 – €195 – £150

NEW
MARIA BY CALLAS
IN HER OWN WORDS
ISBN: 9781614285502
$195 – €195 – £150

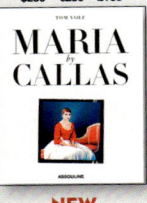

NEW
SEVAN BIÇAKÇI
TIME
ISBN: 9781614286332
$195 – €195 – £150

FRED JOAILLIER FR
ISBN: 9781614285496
$195 – €195 – £150

UNEXPECTED CREATIONS
BY LOTUS ARTS DE VIVRE
ISBN: 9781614285304
$195 – €195 – £150

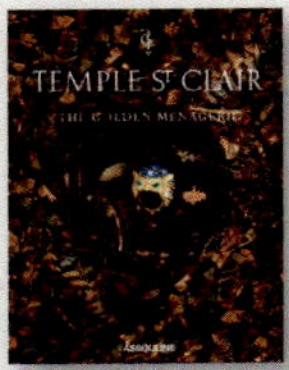

THE GOLDEN MENAGERIE
ISBN: 9781614285427
$195 – €195 – £150

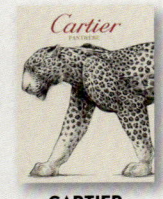

CARTIER PANTHÈRE FR
ISBN: 9781614284284
$195 – €195 – £150

FENDI ROMA
ISBN: 9781614284727
$195 – €195 – £150

VALENTINO
MIRABILIA ROMAE
ISBN: 9781614284406
$250 – €250 – £195

VALENTINO
AT THE EMPEROR'S TABLE
ISBN: 9781614282938
$150 – €150 – £110

CECIL BEATON
ISBN: 9782759404728
$250 – €250 – £195

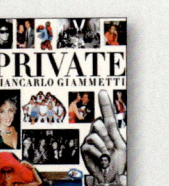

PRIVATE: GIANCARLO GIAMMETTI
ISBN: 9781614281412
$250 – €250 – £195

ELIE SAAB
ISBN: 9781614281016
$250 – €250 – £195

LIFE OF STYLE
BY VINCE CAMUTO
ISBN: 9781614281986
$250 – €250 – £195

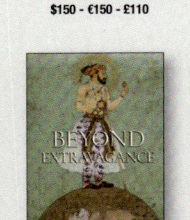

BEYOND EXTRAVAGANCE
A ROYAL COLLECTION OF GEMS AND JEWELS
ISBN: 9781614281290
$250 – €250 – £195

JEWELS OF THE RENAISSANCE
ISBN: 9781614282037
$195 – €195 – £150

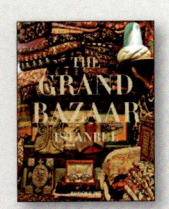

THE GRAND BAZAAR ISTANBUL
ISBN: 9781614280064
$250 – €250 – £195

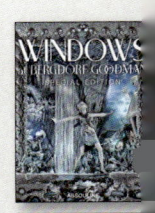

ARCHIVE
WINDOWS AT BERGDORF GOOD
SPECIAL EDITION
ISBN: 978161428082

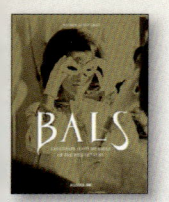

BALS
LEGENDARY COSTUME BALLS
OF THE TWENTIETH CENTURY
ISBN: 9781614280002
$195 - €195 - £150

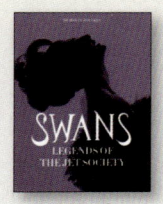

SWANS
LEGENDS OF THE
JET SOCIETY
ISBN: 9781614281283
$195 - €195 - £150

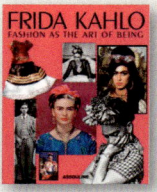

FRIDA KAHLO
FASHION AS THE
ART OF BEING
ISBN: 9781614282631
$195 - €195 - £150

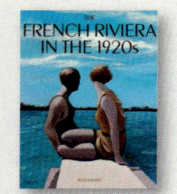

**THE FRENCH RIVIERA
IN THE 1920S**
ISBN: 9782843233661
$195 - €195 - £150

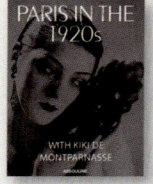

**PARIS IN THE
1920s** FR **WITH KIKI DE
MONTPARNASSE**
ISBN: 9781614280576
$195 - €195 - £150

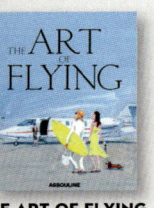

THE ART OF FLYING
ISBN: 9781614284611
$175 - €175 - £135

OSCAR DE LA RENTA
ISBN: 9781614280750
$125 - €125 - £95

SEVAN BIÇAKÇI
ISBN: 9781614281924
$165 - €165 - £130

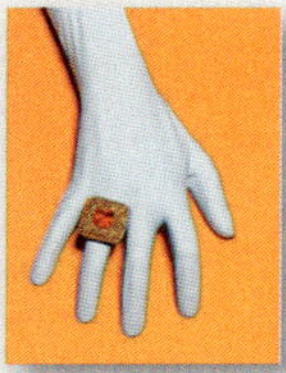

SUZANNE SYZ
ART JEWELS
ISBN: 9781614280873
$150 - €150 - £110

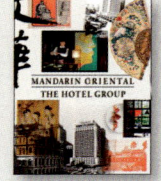

MANDARIN ORIENTAL
ISBN: 9781614284581
$175 - €175 - £135

CROSS PURPOSE
ISBN: 9781614284499
$175 - €175 - £135

H.STERN
ISBN: 9781614284802
$165 - €165 - £130

**HAMPTONS
GARDENS**
ISBN: 9782759405114
$150 - €150 - £110

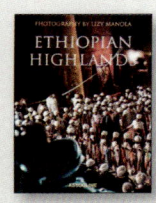

**ETHIOPIAN
HIGHLANDS**
ISBN: 9781614282969
$250 - €250 - £195

GQ MEN
55 YEARS OF LOOKING
SHARP AND LIVING SMART
ISBN: 9781614281450
$150 - €150 - £110

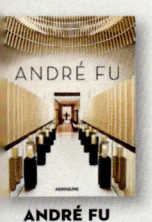

ANDRÉ FU
ISBN: 9781614282860
$165 - €165 - £130

ONE OF 100
MASERATI & ZEGNA
ISBN: 9781614284420
$195 - €195 - £150

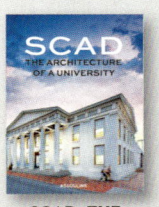

**SCAD: THE
ARCHITECTURE
OF A
UNIVERSITY**
ISBN: 9781614285403
$85 - €80 - £55

**ARCHIVE
NARDI**
ISBN: 9781614280491

**CITY LIGHTS
COLLECTION**

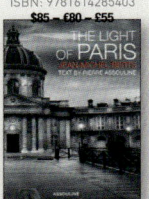

**THE LIGHT OF
PARIS** FR
ISBN: 9782843238819
$75 - €75 - £58

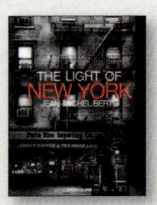

**THE LIGHT OF
NEW YORK** FR
ISBN: 9782759401741
$75 - €75 - £58

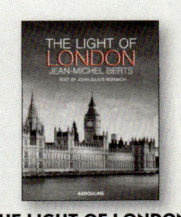

THE LIGHT OF LONDON
FR
ISBN: 9781614280422
$75 - €75 - £58

CITY LIGHTS COLLECTION CONTINUED

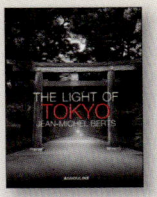

THE LIGHT OF TOKYO FR
ISBN: 9782759403066
$75 – €75 – £58

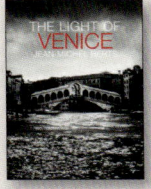

THE LIGHT OF VENICE FR
ISBN: 9781614280231
$75 – €75 – £58

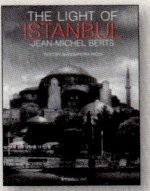

THE LIGHT OF ISTANBUL FR
ISBN: 9781614280309
$75 – €75 – £58

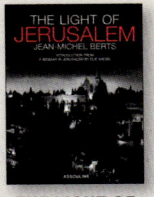

THE LIGHT OF JERUSALEM FR
ISBN: 9781614282082
$75 – €75 – £58

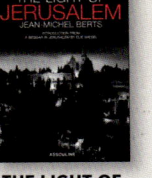

THE LIGHT OF THREE-BOOK SLIPCASE SET
ISBN: 9781614280309
$225 – €225 – £175

CLASSICS COLLECTION
10 x 13 in
25 x 33 cm

NEW
IBIZA BOHEMIA
ISBN: 9781614285915
$85 – €85 – £60

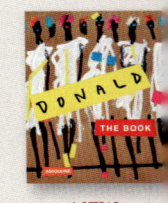

NEW
ASPEN STYLE
ISBN: 9781614286226
$85 – €85 – £60

NEW
DONALD
ISBN: 9781614286301
$85 – €85 – £60

NEW
GIACOBETTI FR
BN: 9781614286165
$85 – €85 – £60

NEW
JOURNEY BY DESIGN
KATHARINE POOLEY
ISBN: 9781614286288
$85 – €85 – £60

NEW
THE BOSPHORUS LIFE
ISBN: 9781614286516
$85 – €85 – £60

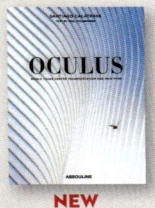

NEW
SANTIAGO CALATRAVA OCULUS
ISBN: 9781614286295
$85 – €85 – £60

HAIR
ISBN: 9781614285113
$85 – €85 – £60

THE ITALIAN DREAM
WINE, HERITAGE, SOUL
ISBN: 9781614285199
$85 – €85 – £60

NOMAD DELUXE
ISBN: 9781614285151
$85 – €85 – £60

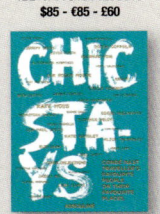

CHIC STAYS CONDÉ NAST TRAVELLER'S FAVOURITE PEOPLE ON THEIR FAVOURITE PLACES
ISBN: 9781614285373
$85 – €85 – £60

ORIENT EXPRESS FR
ORIGINS OF THE ART OF TRAVEL
ISBN: 9781614285458
$85 – €85 – £60

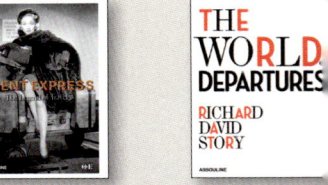

THE WORLD OF DEPARTURES
ISBN: 9781614282658
$85 – €85 – £60

THE PEARL NECKLACE
ISBN: 9781614285120
$85 – €85 – £60

FLOWERS FR
ART & BOUQUETS
ISBN: 9781614285144
$85 – €85 – £60

LA COLLECTION PRIVÉE CHRISTIAN DIOR FR
ISBN: 9781614284635
$95 – €95 – £70

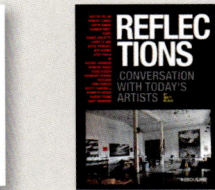

REFLECTIONS BY MATT BLACK
IN CONVERSATION WITH TODAY'S ARTISTS
ISBN: 9781614285359
$85 – €85 – £60

VEUVE CLICQUOT
ISBN: 9781614285539
$85 – €85 – £60

THE BIG BOOK OF CHIC
BY MILES REDD
ISBN: 9781614280613
$85 – €85 – £60

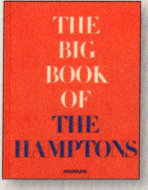

THE BIG BOOK OF THE HAMPTONS
ISBN: 9781614282273
$85 – €85 – £60

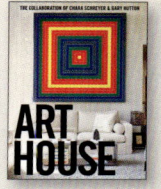

ART HOUSE
THE COLLABORATION OF CHARA SCHREYER & GARY HUTTON
ISBN: 9781614285366
$85 – €85 – £60

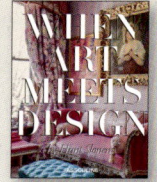

WHEN ART MEETS DESIGN
ISBN: 9781614282877
$85 – €85 – £60

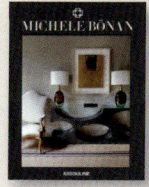

MICHELE BÖNAN
ISBN: 9781614284680
$85 – €85 – £60

RAJASTHAN STYLE FR
ISBN: 9781614284659
$85 – €85 – £60

OTTOMAN CHIC
ISBN: 9781614282662
$85 – €85 – £60

VENETIAN CHIC
ISBN: 9781614285380
$85 – €85 – £60

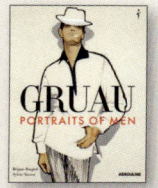

GRUAU FR
PORTRAITS OF MEN
ISBN: 9781614280781
$85 – €85 – £60

A TOUCH OF STYLE
BY CARLOS MOTA
ISBN: 9781614282990
$85 – €85 – £60

BACKSTAGE CIRQUE DU SOLEIL FR
ISBN: 9781614282976
$85 – €85 – £60

GAIA FR
ISBN: 9782759405343
$75 – €75 – £58

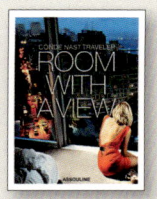

CONDÉ NAST TRAVELER ROOM WITH A VIEW
ISBN: 9782759404476
$75 – €75 – £58

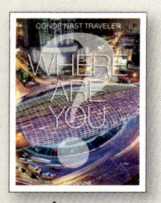

CONDÉ NAST TRAVELER WHERE ARE YOU?
ISBN: 9782759405152
$75 – €75 – £58

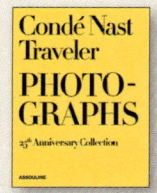

CONDÉ NAST TRAVELER PHOTOGRAPHS: 25TH ANNIVERSARY COLLECTION
ISBN: 9781614280415
$95 – €95 – £70

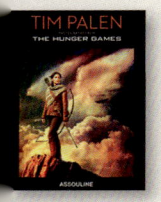

TIM PALEN: PHOTOGRAPHS FROM THE HUNGER GAMES
ISBN: 9781614284444
$75 – €75 – £58

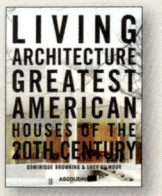

LIVING ARCHITECTURE
GREATEST AMERICAN HOUSES OF THE 20TH CENTURY
ISBN: 9782759404704
$85 – €85 – £60

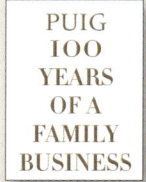

PUIG 100 YEARS OF A FAMILY BUSINESS FR
ISBN: 9781614281900
$85 – €85 – £60

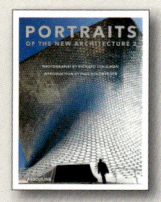

PORTRAITS OF THE NEW ARCHITECTURE 2
ISBN: 9781614282679
$75 – €75 – £58

ARCHIVE
PORTRAITS OF THE NEW ARCHITECTURE
ISBN: 9782843235733

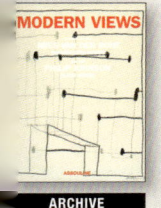

ARCHIVE
MODERN VIEWS
HOMAGE TO MIES VAN DER ROHE AND PHILIP JOHNSON
ISBN: 9782759404674

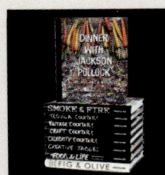

CONNOISSEUR COLLECTION
9.5 x 11.75 in
23.5 x 30 cm

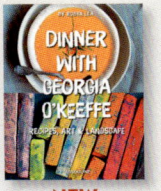

NEW
DINNER WITH GEORGIA O'KEEFFE
RECIPES, ART & LANDSCAPE
ISBN: 9781614285908
$50 - €50 - £38

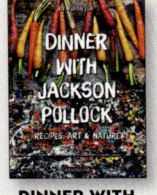

DINNER WITH JACKSON POLLOCK
RECIPES, ART & NATURE
ISBN: 9781614284321
$50 - €50 - £38

SMOKE & FIRE
RECIPES AND MENUS FOR ENTERTAINING OUTDOORS
ISBN: 9781614285168
$50 - €50 - £38

VINTAGE COCKTAILS FR
ISBN: 9782759404131
$50 - €50 - £38

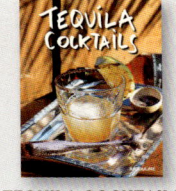

TEQUILA COCKTAILS
ISBN: 9781614285441
$50 - €50 - £38

CELEBRITY COCKTAILS
ISBN: 9781614282587
$50 - €50 - £38

CRAFT COCKTAILS
ISBN: 9781614281030
$50 - €50 - £38

CREATIVE TABLES
ISBN: 9781614285434
$50 - €50 - £38

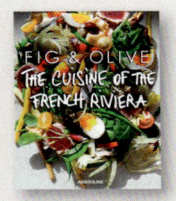

FIG & OLIVE
THE CUISINE OF THE FRENCH RIVIERA
ISBN: 9781614284567
$50 - €50 - £38

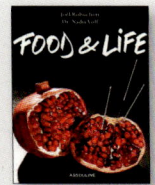

FOOD & LIFE FR
JOËL ROBUCHON AND DR. NADIA VOLF
ISBN: 9781614282648
$50 - €50 - £38

ICONS COLLECTION
7.5 x 11 in
19.5 x 28 cm

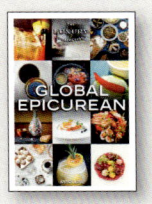

NEW
THE LUXURY COLLECTION GLOBAL EPICUREAN
ISBN: 9781614285922
$50 - €50 - £38

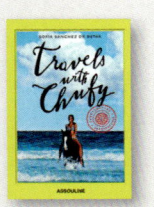

NEW
TRAVELS WITH CHUFY
ISBN: 9781614285939
$50 - €50 - £38

NEW
COVA
ISBN: 9781614286615
$50 - €50 - £38

NEW
COCKTAIL CHAMELEON
ISBN: 9781614286196
$50 - €50 - £38

NEW
TRANSFORM
60 MAKEUP LOOKS BY TONI MALT
ISBN: 9781614286608
$50 - €50 - £38

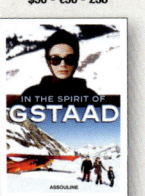

IN THE SPIRIT OF GSTAAD
ISBN: 9781614284741
$50 - €50 - £38

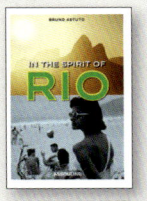

IN THE SPIRIT OF RIO FR
ISBN: 9781614285328
$50 - €50 - £38

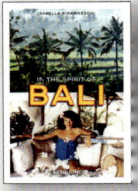

IN THE SPIRIT OF BALI
ISBN: 9781614285182
$50 - €50 - £38

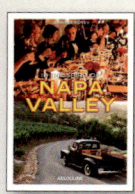

IN THE SPIRIT OF NAPA VALLEY
ISBN: 9781614284390
$50 - €50 - £38

IN THE SPIRIT OF CAPRI FR
ISBN: 9782759404063
$50 - €50 - £38

IN THE SPIRIT OF MONTE CARLO
ISBN: 9781614282136
$50 - €50 - £38

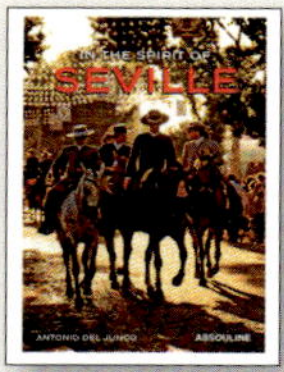

IN THE SPIRIT OF SEVILLE FR
ISBN: 9781614281481
$50 - €50 - £38

IN THE SPIRIT OF PALM BEACH
ISBN: 9781614280606
$50 - €50 - £38

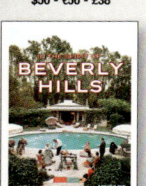

IN THE SPIRIT OF BEVERLY HILLS
ISBN: 9781614281542
$50 - €50 - £38

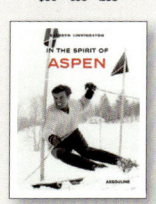

IN THE SPIRIT OF ASPEN
ISBN: 9782843233999
$50 - €50 - £38

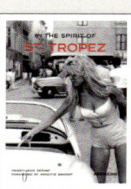

IN THE SPIRIT OF ST. TROPEZ FR
ISBN: 9782843235061
$50 - €50 - £38

IN THE SPIRIT OF ST. BARTHS
ISBN: 9782759405176
$50 - €50 - £38

IN THE SPIRIT OF MIAMI BEACH
ISBN: 9782843238796
$50 - €50 - £38

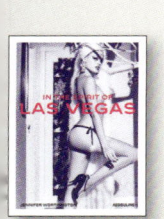

IN THE SPIRIT OF LAS VEGAS
ISBN: 9782759401153
$50 - €50 - £38

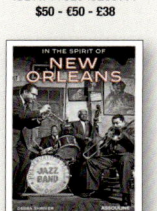

IN THE SPIRIT OF NEW ORLEANS FR
ISBN: 9781614280590
$50 - €50 - £38

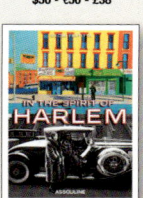

IN THE SPIRIT OF HARLEM
ISBN: 9781614281498
$50 - €50 - £38

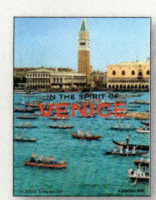

IN THE SPIRIT OF VENICE FR
ISBN: 9782843236631
$50 - €50 - £38

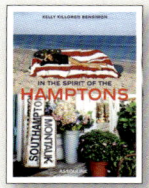

IN THE SPIRIT OF THE HAMPTONS
ISBN: 9781614281399
$50 - €50 - £38

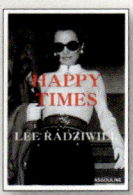

HAPPY TIMES
ISBN: 9782843232503
$50 - €50 - £38

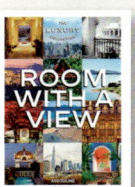

THE LUXURY COLLECTION ROOM WITH A VIEW
ISBN: 9781614285090
$50 - €50 - £38

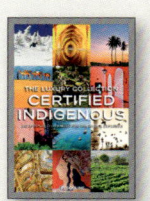

THE LUXURY COLLECTION CERTIFIED INDIGENOUS
ISBN: 9781614284376
$50 - €50 - £38

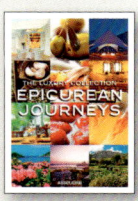

THE LUXURY COLLECTION EPICUREAN JOURNEYS
ISBN: 9781614281894
$50 - €50 - £38

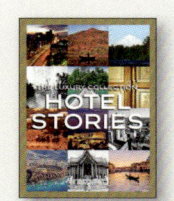

THE LUXURY COLLECTION HOTEL STORIES
ISBN: 9781614281320
$50 - €50 - £38

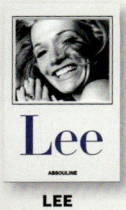

LEE
ISBN: 9781614284697
$50 - €50 - £38

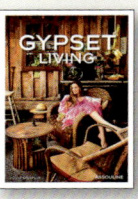

GYPSET LIVING
ISBN: 9781614282112
$50 - €50 - £38

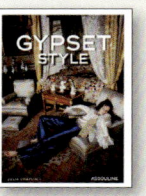

GYPSET STYLE
ISBN: 9782759403967
$50 - €50 - £38

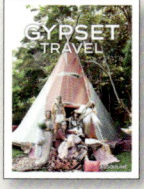

GYPSET TRAVEL
ISBN: 9781614280620
$50 - €50 - £38

GYPSET TRILOGY SLIPCASE SET
ISBN: 9781614282921
$140 - €140 - £105

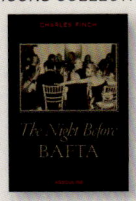

ICONS COLLECTION CONTINUED

THE NIGHT BEFORE BAFTA
ISBN: 9781614285137
$50 – €50 – £38

VOLEZ, VOGUEZ, VOYAGEZ FR
BY LOUIS VUITTON MALLETIER
ISBN: 9781614285342
$50 – €50 – £38

#CARLOS'S PLACES
ISBN: 9781614282440
$50 – €50 – £38

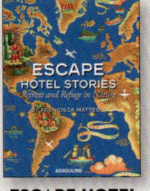

ESCAPE HOTEL STORIES FR
RETREAT AND REFUGE IN NATURE
ISBN: 9781614280477
$50 – €50 – £38

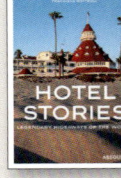

HOTEL STORIES FR
ISBN: 9782843233425
$50 – €50 – £38

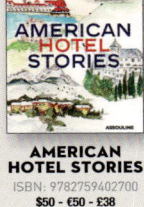

AMERICAN HOTEL STORIES
ISBN: 9782759402700
$50 – €50 – £38

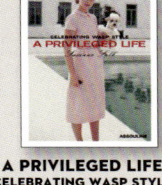

A PRIVILEGED LIFE
CELEBRATING WASP STYLE
ISBN: 9782759401260
$50 – €50 – £38

HITCHCOCK STYLE FR
ISBN: 9782843235146
$50 – €50 – £38

DOLCE VITA STYLE FR
ISBN: 9782843237317
$50 – €50 – £38

PUTMAN STYLE FR
ISBN: 9782843236693
$50 – €50 – £38

SOUTH POLE
THE BRITISH ANTARCTIC EXPEDITION 1910-1913
ISBN: 9781614280101
$50 – €50 – £38

FRENCH RIVIERA FR
ISBN: 9782843233661
$50 – €50 – £38

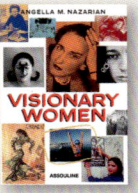

VISIONARY WOMEN
ISBN: 9781614284550
$50 – €50 – £38

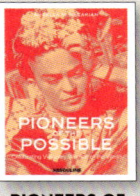

PIONEERS OF THE POSSIBLE
CELEBRATING VISIONARY WOMEN OF THE WORLD
ISBN: 9781614280392
$50 – €50 – £38

TO INDIA WITH LOVE
FROM NEW YORK TO MUMBAI
ISBN: 9782759404216
$50 – €50 – £38

GEOFFREY BEENE
ISBN: 9782759402663
$50 – €50 – £38

DRESSING FOR THE DARK
ISBN: 9781614282594
$50 – €50 – £38

THE SCHOOL OF FASHION
ISBN: 9781614282051
$50 – €50 – £38

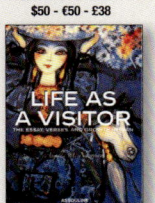

ARCHIVE
LIFE AS A VISITOR
ISBN: 9782759404070

ARCHIVE
BE MY GUEST
ISBN: 9782843233456

ARCHIVE
WATCHES FR
THE ULTIMATE GUIDE
ISBN: 9782759404162

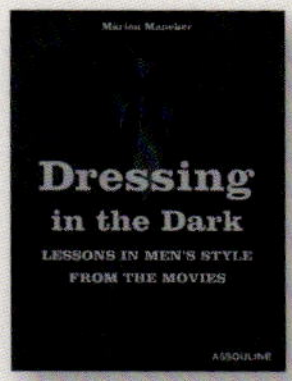

ARCHIVE
DRESSING IN THE DARK
ISBN: 9782843233616

ARCHIVE
TIME BY CHANEL FR
ISBN: 9782843235115

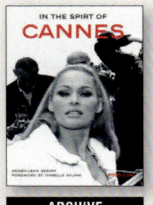

ARCHIVE
IN THE SPIRIT OF CANNES FR
ISBN: 9782843236105

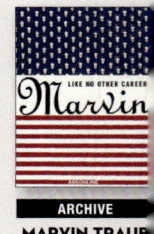

ARCHIVE
MARVIN TRAUB
LIKE NO OTHER CAREER
ISBN: 9782759402724

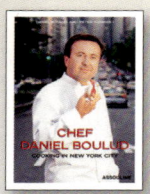

ARCHIVE	ARCHIVE	ARCHIVE	ARCHIVE	ARCHIVE
CHEF DANIEL BOULUD	**ROYAL HOLIDAYS** FR	**PALM SPRINGS STYLE**	**ISLAND HOTEL STORIES**	**PARIS HOTEL STORIES** FR
ISBN: 9782843233708	ISBN: 9782843235085	ISBN: 9782843237430	ISBN: 9782843234484	ISBN: 9782843233685

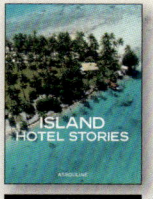

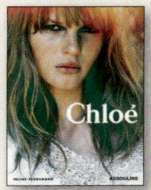

MÉMOIRE COLLECTION
FASHION
6 x 8.5 in
15.5 x 21.5 cm

CHANEL FR THREE-BOOK SLIPCASE SET	**DIOR** FR THREE-BOOK SLIPCASE SET	**LOUIS VUITTON ICONS** FR
ISBN: 9782843235184	ISBN: 9781614280200	ISBN: 9782843239038
$25 - €25 - £18	$75 - €75 - £58	$25 - €25 - £18

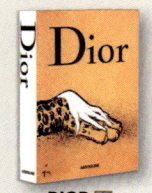

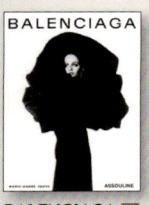

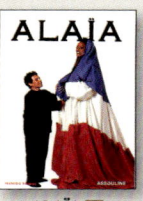

BALENCIAGA FR	**CHLOÉ** FR	**ALAÏA** FR	**THE LITTLE BLACK DRESS** FR	**YVES SAINT LAURENT** FR
ISBN: 9782843236242	ISBN: 9782843234378	ISBN: 9782843238963	ISBN: 9782843232893	ISBN: 9782759402564
$25 - €25 - £18	$25 - €25 - £18	$25 - €25 - £18	$25 - €25 - £18	$25 - €25 - £18

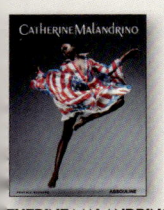

THERINE MALANDRINO	**ROGER VIVIER** FR	**DIANE VON FURSTENBERG THE WRAP** FR	**LE PLIAGE BY LONGCHAMP** FR	**JEAN PAUL GAULTIER** FR
ISBN: 9782759401680	ISBN: 9782843236754	ISBN: 9782843235245	ISBN: 9781614282952	ISBN: 9782843237126
$25 - €25 - £18	$25 - €25 - £18	$25 - €25 - £18	$25 - €25 - £18	$25 - €25 - £18

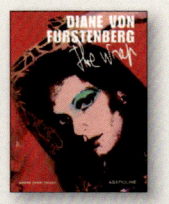

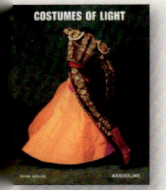

STUMES OF LIGHT FR	**ELIE SAAB**	**MARC JACOBS** FR	**LORIS AZZARO** FR	**COURRÈGES** FR
ISBN: 9782843235832	ISBN: 9781614281009	ISBN: 9782843236303	ISBN: 9781614280217	ISBN: 9782843236266
$25 - €25 - £18	$25 - €25 - £18	$25 - €25 - £18	$25 - €25 - £18	$25 - €25 - £18

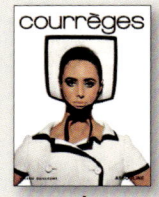

MÉMOIRE COLLECTION: FASHION CONTINUED

EMILIO PUCCI
ISBN: 9782843236006
$25 - €25 - £18

NANCY GONZALEZ
ISBN: 9781614280835
$25 - €25 - £18

FRED ASTAIRE STYLE FR
ISBN: 9782843236778
$25 - €25 - £18

REBEL STYLE FR
ISBN: 9782843237515
$25 - €25 - £18

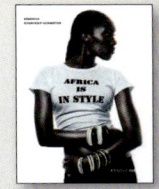

AFRICA IS IN STYLE
ISBN: 9782843238000
$25 - €25 - £18

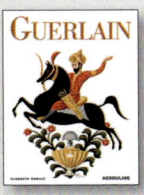

GUERLAIN FR
ISBN: 9782843234125
$25 - €25 - £18

FASHION DOGS FR
ISBN: 9782843233401
$25 - €25 - £18

ARCHIVE
BARBIE FR
ISBN: 9782843237720

ARCHIVE
CHARLES JAMES FR
ISBN: 9782843238970

ARCHIVE
CUFF LINKS FR
ISBN: 9782843233388

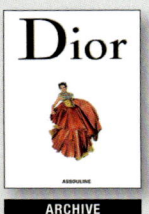

ARCHIVE
DIOR FR
ISBN: 9782843236761

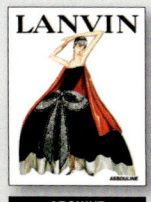

ARCHIVE
LANVIN FR
ISBN: 9782759401017

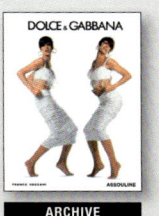

ARCHIVE
DOLCE & GABBANA FR
ISBN: 9782843237751

ARCHIVE
COACH
ISBN: 9782843234279

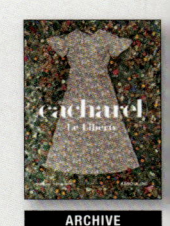

ARCHIVE
CACHAREL LE LIBERTY FR
ISBN: 9782843234033

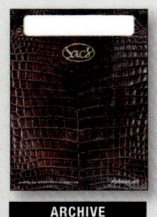

ARCHIVE
BAGS FR
ISBN: 9782843234538

ARCHIVE
HELENA RUBINSTEIN FR
ISBN: 9782843234262

ARCHIVE
GRÈS FR
ISBN: 9782843234163

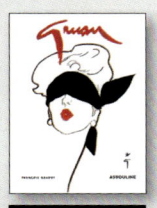

ARCHIVE
GRUAU FR
ISBN: 9782843234156

ARCHIVE
GOTTEX FR
ISBN: 9782843238727

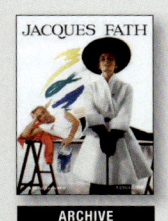

ARCHIVE
JACQUES FATH FR
ISBN: 9782759403912

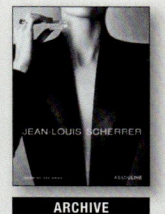

ARCHIVE
JEAN-LOUIS SCHERRER FR
ISBN: 9782759401437

ARCHIVE
MCM
ISBN: 9782759404223

ARCHIVE
PHILIP TREACY FR
ISBN: 9782843233722

ARCHIVE
POIRET FR
ISBN: 9782759401000

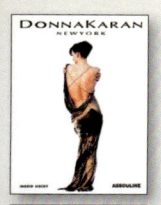

ARCHIVE	ARCHIVE	ARCHIVE	ARCHIVE	ARCHIVE
DONNA KARAN FR	**ROBERTO CAVALLI** FR	**FASHION & SURREALISM** FR	**RUFFIAN INSIDE OUT**	**SERGIO ROSSI** FR
ISBN: 9782843237133	ISBN: 9782843233920	ISBN: 9782843233784	ISBN: 9782759403998	ISBN: 9782759401703

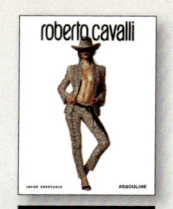

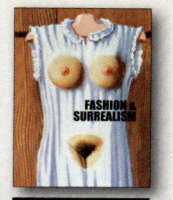

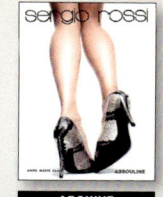

ARCHIVE	ARCHIVE	ARCHIVE	ARCHIVE	ARCHIVE
SOLSTISS	**TENNIS FASHION** FR	**TIES** FR	**TOPOLINO** FR	**YOHJI YAMAMOTO** FR
ISBN: 9782843239489	ISBN: 9782843234385	ISBN: 9782843235238	ISBN: 9782843233715	ISBN: 9782843237041

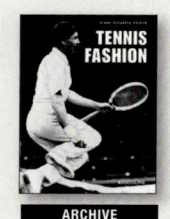

ART

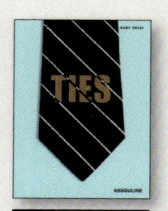

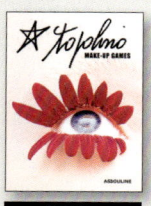

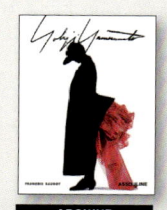

ARCHIVE				
THE LITTLE BLACK DRESS DIET FR	**AI WEIWEI**	**CÉZANNE IN PROVENCE** FR	**FARFETCH CURATES ART**
ISBN: 9782759401123	ISBN: 9781614281917	ISBN: 9782843236518	ISBN: 9781614284482
	$25 - €25 - £18	$25 - €25 - £18	$25 - €25 - £18

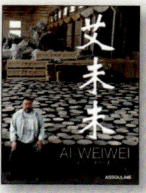

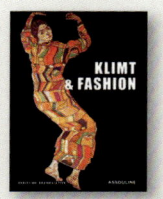

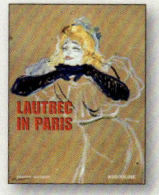

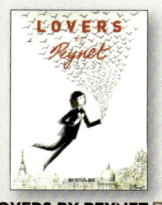

GEISHAS FR	**KLIMT & FASHION** FR	**LAUTREC IN PARIS** FR	**LOVERS BY PEYNET** FR	**MONA LISA AN ENIGMA** FR
ISBN: 9782843234231	ISBN: 9782843234170	ISBN: 9782843236556	ISBN: 9782759405268	ISBN: 9782843236532
$25 - €25 - £18	$25 - €25 - £18	$25 - €25 - £18	$25 - €25 - £18	$25 - €25 - £18

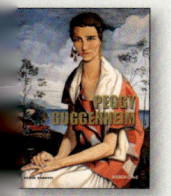

	ARCHIVE	ARCHIVE	ARCHIVE	ARCHIVE
PEGGY GUGGENHEIM FR	**PICABIA**	**PICASSO THE OBJECTS** FR	**MIRÓ'S STUDIO** FR	**THE DADA SPIRIT** FR
ISBN: 9782843236594	ISBN: 9782843234040	ISBN: 9782843234255	ISBN: 9782843236259	ISBN: 9782843234187
$25 - €25 - £18				

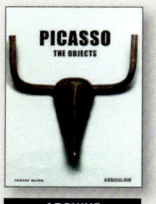

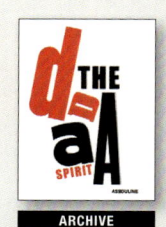

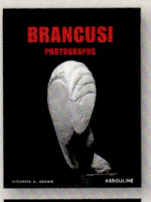

MÉMOIRE COLLECTION: ART CONTINUED

ARCHIVE
BRANCUSI PHOTOGRAPHS FR
ISBN: 9782843234095

ARCHIVE
GREEK BEAUTY FR
ISBN: 9782843235511

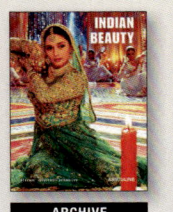

ARCHIVE
INDIAN BEAUTY FR
ISBN: 9782843235726

ARCHIVE
JEAN COCTEAU FR
ISBN: 9782843236037

ARCHIVE
DIEGO GIACOMETTI FR
ISBN: 9782843232992

ARCHIVE
BALTHUS FR
ISBN: 9782843233012

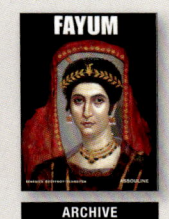

ARCHIVE
FAYUM
ISBN: 9782843236280

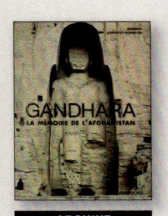

ARCHIVE
GANDHARA
ISBN: 9782843232947

ARCHIVE
GAUGUIN NOA NOA
ISBN: 9782843235627

ARCHIVE
CHEMA MADOZ FR
ISBN: 9782843231544

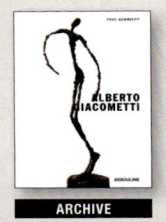

ARCHIVE
ALBERTO GIACOMETTI FR
ISBN: 9782843233005

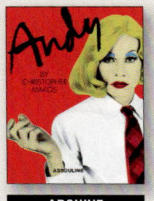

ARCHIVE
ANDY FR
ISBN: 9782843232794

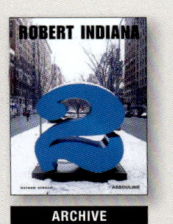

ARCHIVE
ROBERT INDIANA FR
ISBN: 9782843235252

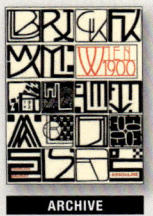

ARCHIVE
VIENNA 1900 FR
ISBN: 9782843238178

DESIGN & ARCHITECTURE

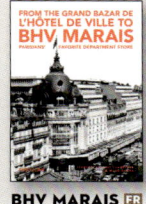

BHV MARAIS FR
ISBN: 9782759407521
$25 - €25 - £18

BAUHAUS FR
ISBN: 9782843234149
$25 - €25 - £18

J. M. FRANK FR
ISBN: 9782843236273
$25 - €25 - £18

CHARLOTTE PERRIAND FR
ISBN: 9782843236617
$25 - €25 - £18

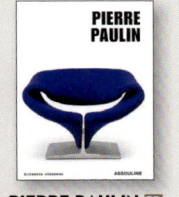

PIERRE PAULIN FR
ISBN: 9782843235672
$25 - €25 - £18

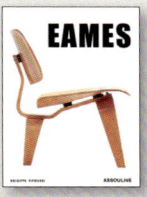

EAMES
ISBN: 9782843234200
$25 - €25 - £18

EILEEN GRAY FR
ISBN: 9782843236013
$25 - €25 - £18

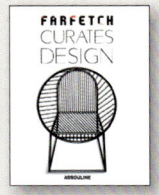

FARFETCH CURATES DESIGN
ISBN: 9781614284475
$25 - €25 - £18

MORRIS LAPIDUS
ISBN: 9782843236297
$25 - €25 - £18

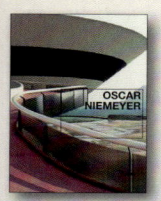

OSCAR NIEMEYER
ISBN: 9782843233449
$25 - €25 - £18

RAYMOND LOEWY FR
ISBN: 9782843237744
$25 - €25 - £18

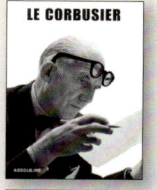

ARCHIVE
LE CORBUSIER
ISBN: 9782843234194

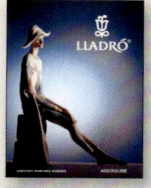

ARCHIVE
LLADRÓ
ISBN: 9782843238680

ARCHIVE
MILLER HOUSE AND GARDEN
ISBN: 9781614230019

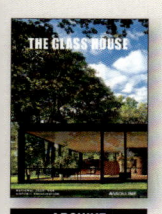

ARCHIVE
THE GLASS HOUSE
ISBN: 9782759401673

ARCHIVE
FORNASETTI FR
ISBN: 9782843236792

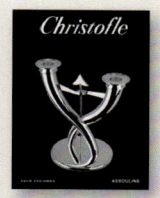

ARCHIVE
CHRISTOFLE FR
ISBN: 9782843236570

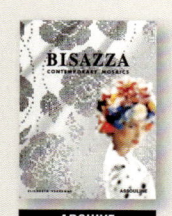

ARCHIVE
BISAZZA FR
ISBN: 9782843238703

JEWELRY

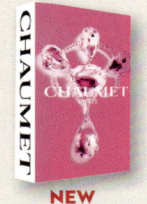

NEW
CHAUMET FR
PHOTOGRAPHY, ARTS, FETES
THREE-BOOK SLIPCASE SET
ISBN: 9781614285311
$75 - €75 - £58

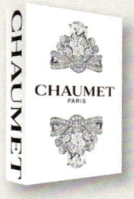

CHAUMET FR
PLACE VENDÔME, TIARAS, NATURALISM
THREE-BOOK SLIPCASE SET
ISBN: 9781614285311
$75 - €75 - £58

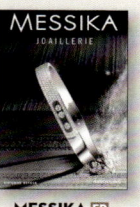

MESSIKA FR
ISBN: 9781614285274
$25 - €25 - £18

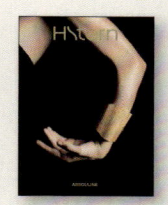

H.STERN
ISBN: 9781614284819
$25 - €25 - £18

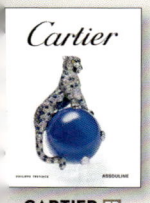

CARTIER FR
ISBN: 9782843236747
$25 - €25 - £18

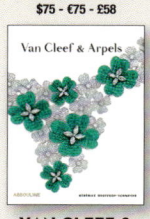

VAN CLEEF & ARPELS FR
ISBN: 9781614282181
$25 - €25 - £18

CODOGNATO FR
ISBN: 9782843234002
$25 - €25 - £18

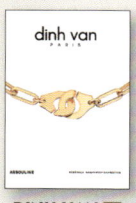

DINH VAN FR
ISBN: 9781614284673
$25 - €25 - £18

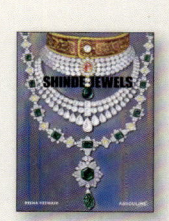

SHINDE JEWELS
ISBN: 9782843235702
$25 - €25 - £18

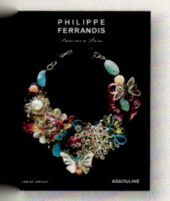

IPPE FERRANDIS FR
ISBN: 9781614281696
$25 - €25 - £18

ARCHIVE
LÉON HATOT FR
ISBN: 9782843234712

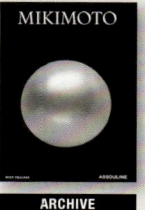

ARCHIVE
MIKIMOTO
ISBN: 9782759402588

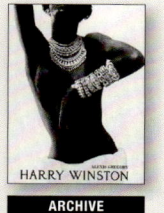

ARCHIVE
HARRY WINSTON FR
ISBN: 9782759404292

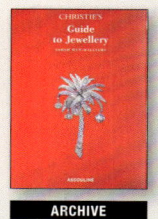

ARCHIVE
CHRISTIE'S GUIDE TO JEWELLERY FR
ISBN: 9782843233029

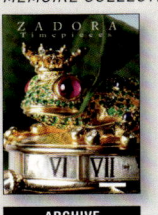

MÉMOIRE COLLECTION: JEWELRY CONTINUED

STYLE

ARCHIVE
ZADORA TIMEPIECES
ISBN: 9782759401765

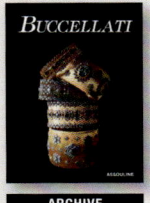

ARCHIVE
BUCCELLATI FR
ISBN: 9782843233739

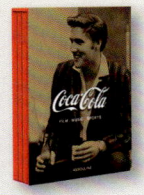

COCA-COLA FR
THREE-BOOK SET
ISBN: 9781614281436
$75 - €75 - £58

CIGAR STYLE
ISBN: 9782759402687
$25 - €25 - £18

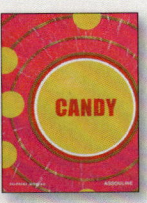

CANDY FR
ISBN: 9782843237492
$25 - €25 - £18

FARFETCH CURATES FOOD
ISBN: 9781614284369
$25 - €25 - £18

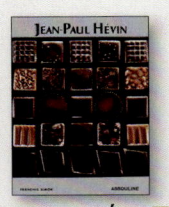

JEAN-PAUL HÉVIN FR
ISBN: 9782759402571
$25 - €25 - £18

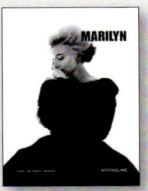

MARILYN
ISBN: 9782843233951
$25 - €25 - £18

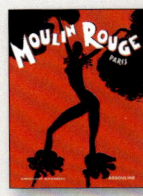

MOULIN ROUGE FR
ISBN: 9782843235504
$25 - €25 - £18

YELLOW: VEUVE CLIQUOT
ISBN: 9782759402533
$25 - €25 - £18

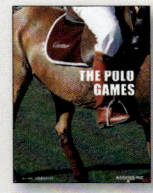

THE POLO GAMES
ISBN: 9782843239526
$25 - €25 - £18

MARIE-ANTOINETTE STYLE FR
ISBN: 9782843237539
$25 - €25 - £18

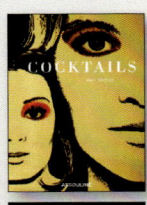

ARCHIVE
COCKTAILS
ISBN: 9782843237478

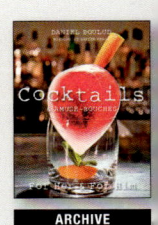

ARCHIVE
DANIEL BOULUD COCKTAILS & AMUSE-BOUCHES
ISBN: 9781614280026

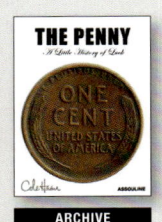

ARCHIVE
THE PENNY
A LITTLE HISTORY OF LUCK
ISBN: 9782759403042

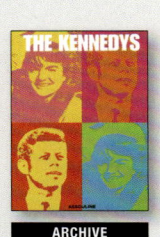

ARCHIVE
THE KENNEDYS
TWO-BOOK SET:
JACKIE & JFK
ISBN: 9782843237874

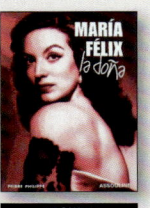

ARCHIVE
MARÍA FÉLIX FR
LA DOÑA
ISBN: 9782843238888

RELIGION

SYMBOLS OF TIBETAN BUDDHISM FR
ISBN: 9782843235009
$25 - €25 - £18

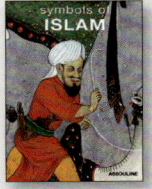

SYMBOLS OF ISLAM FR
ISBN: 9782843231995
$25 - €25 - £18

ARCHIVE
SYMBOLS OF JUDAISM FR
ISBN: 9782843231988

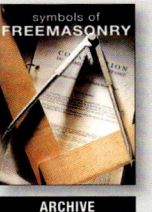

ARCHIVE
SYMBOLS OF FREEMASONRY FR
ISBN: 9782843232015

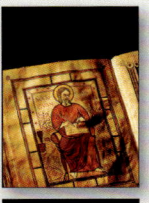

ARCHIVE
SYMBOLS OF CATHOLICISM FR
ISBN: 9782843231889

OTHER FORMATS

ART FOLIO COLLECTION
13 x 16.5 in
32 x 42 cm

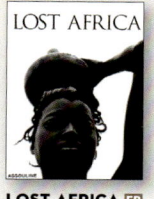

LOST AFRICA FR
ISBN: 9782843236075
$250 - €250 - £195

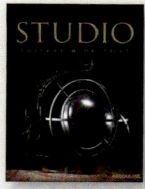

STUDIO
ISBN: 9782759403028
$250 - €250 - £195

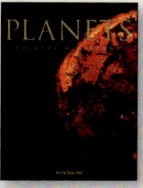

PLANETS
ISBN: 9782759403837
$250 - €250 - £195

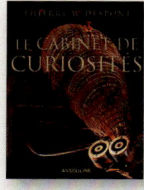

LE CABINET DE CURIOSITÉS
ISBN: 9781614280729
$150 - €150 - £110

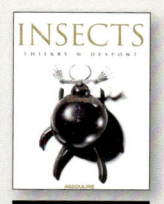

ARCHIVE
INSECTS
ISBN: 9782759403011

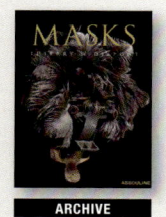

ARCHIVE
MASKS
ISBN: 9782759401154

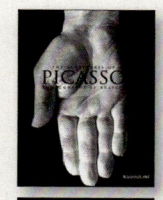

ARCHIVE
THE SCULPTURES OF PICASSO FR
ISBN: 9782843237881

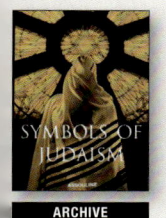

ARCHIVE
SYMBOLS OF JUDAISM FR
ISBN: 9782843237898

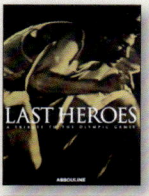

ARCHIVE
LAST HEROES
A TRIBUTE TO THE OLYMPIC GAMES
ISBN: 9782843235856

GAME BOOK COLLECTION
6 x 8.5 in
15.5 x 21.5 cm

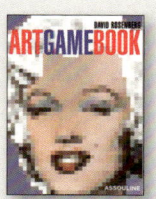

ART GAME BOOK FR
ISBN: 9782759404834
$50 - €50 - £38

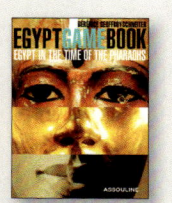

EGYPT GAME BOOK FR
ISBN: 9782759401758
$50 - €50 - £38

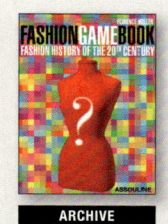

ARCHIVE
FASHION GAME BOOK FR
ISBN: 9782759402922

ARCHIVE
SIC GAME BOOK FR
SBN: 9782843238277

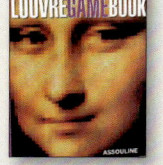

ARCHIVE
LOUVRE GAME BOOK FR
ISBN: 9782843237331

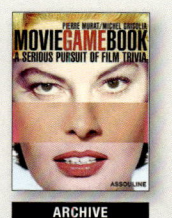

ARCHIVE
MOVIE GAME BOOK FR
ISBN: 9782843236051

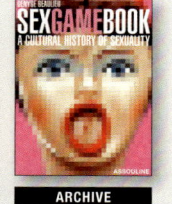

ARCHIVE
SEX GAME BOOK FR
ISBN: 9782759401079

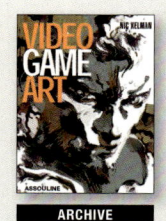

ARCHIVE
VIDEO GAME ART FR
ISBN: 9782843237294

ART
DESIGN
ARCHITECTURE

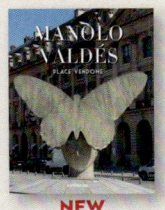

NEW
MANOLO VALDÉS
PLACE VENDÔME
ISBN: 9781614285960
$95 - €95 - £70

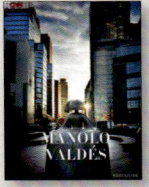

MANOLO VALDÉS
ISBN: 9781614280033
$95 - €95 - £70

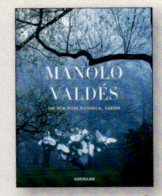

MANOLO VALDÉS
MONUMENTAL SCULPTURE AT THE
NEW YORK BOTANICAL GARDEN
ISBN: 9781614281467
$95 - €95 - £70

ARCHITECT OF DREAMS
LA MODE EN IMAGES
BY OLIVIER MASSART **FR**
ISBN: 9781614280941
$95 - €95 - £70

RENZO MONGIARDINO
RENAISSANCE MASTER
OF STYLE **FR**
ISBN: 9781614281023
$95 - €95 - £70

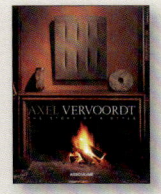

AXEL VERVOORDT FR
THE STORY OF A STYLE
ISBN: 9782843232978
$95 - €95 - £70

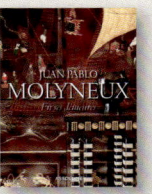

**JUAN PABLO
MOLYNEUX**
AT HOME **FR**
ISBN: 9781614285205
$95 - €95 - £70

**ABCDCS: DAVID
COLLINS STUDIO**
ISBN: 9781614282297
$85 - €85 - £60

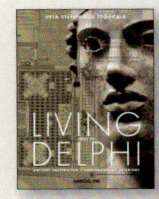

**LIVING NEXT
TO DELPHI**
ISBN: 9781614281566
$75 - €70 - £50

**KISS THE
PAST HELLO**
ISBN: 9781614284437
$65 - €65 - £55

COCA-COLA FR
ISBN: 9782759405145
$65 - €65 - £55

MATTEL
70 YEARS OF
INNOVATION AND PLAY
ISBN: 9781614284604
$125 - €125 - £95

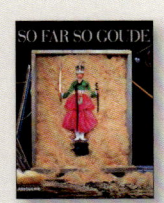

SO FAR SO GOUDE
ISBN: 9782843237553
$95 - €95 - £70

HYUNDAI
LIVE BRILLIANT
ISBN: 9781614284451
$125 - €125 - £95

**BRANCUSI
NEW YORK**
ISBN: 9781614281962
$95 - €95 - £70

LOST FISH FR
ISBN: 9782759403929
$65 - €65 - £55

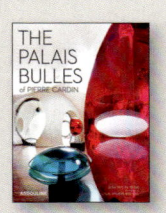

THE PALAIS BULLES FR
OF PIERRE CARDIN
ISBN: 9781614280804
$85 - €85 - £60

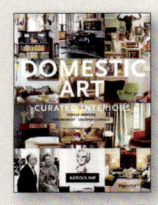

DOMESTIC ART
CURATED INTERIORS
ISBN: 9782759403035
$75 - €70 - £50

LE ROY SOLEIL FR
ISBN: 9782843237805
$95 - €95 - £70

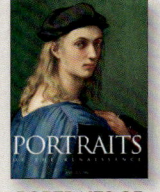

**PORTRAITS OF
THE RENAISSANCE FR**
ISBN: 9782843238901
$125 - €125 - £95

SADE FR
ISBN: 9781614282020
$75 - €70 - £50

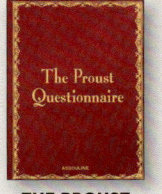

**THE PROUST
QUESTIONNAIRE FR**
ISBN: 9782843236716
$50 - €50 - £38

POLO
THE NOMADIC TRIBE
ISBN: 9782759404100
$125 - €125 - £95

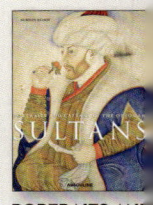

**PORTRAITS AND
CAFTANS OF THE
OTTOMAN SULTANS**
ISBN: 9781614281108
$125 - €125 - £95

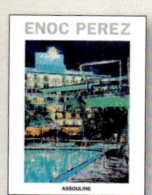

ENOC PEREZ
ISBN: 9781614281528
$95 — €95 — £70

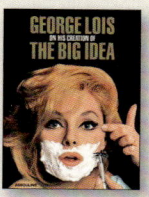

GEORGE LOIS
ON HIS CREATION OF THE BIG IDEA
ISBN: 9782759402991
$75 — €70 — £50

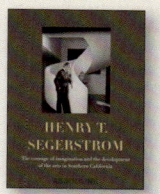

HENRY T. SEGERSTROM
ISBN: 9781614281047
$150 — €150 — £110

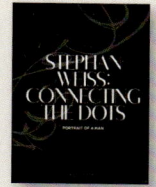

STEPHAN WEISS
CONNECTING THE DOTS
ISBN: 9781614280408
$95 — €95 — £70

VATICAN FR
ISBN: 9782759403936
$75 — €70 — £50

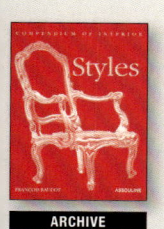

ARCHIVE
COMPENDIUM OF INTERIOR STYLES
ISBN: 9782843237201

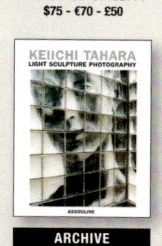

ARCHIVE
KEIICHI TAHARA FR
LIGHT, SCULPTURE, PHOTOGRAPHY
ISBN: 9782843232626

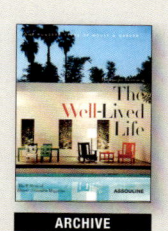

ARCHIVE
THE WELL-LIVED LIFE
ISBN: 9782843234453

ARCHIVE
BARBIE FR
ISBN: 9782759404735

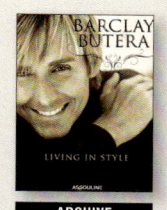

ARCHIVE
BARCLAY BUTERA
LIVING IN STYLE
ISBN: 9782759402878

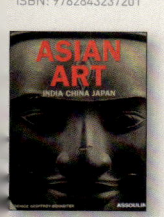

ARCHIVE
ASIAN ART
INDIA CHINA JAPAN
ISBN: 9782843233654

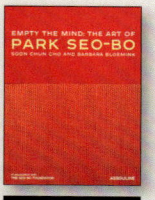

ARCHIVE
EMPTY THE MIND
THE ART OF PARK SEO-BO
ISBN: 9782759403141

ARCHIVE
LOST DIVAS
ISBN: 9782843237355

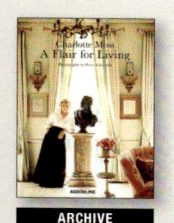

ARCHIVE
CHARLOTTE MOSS
A FLAIR FOR LIVING
ISBN: 9782759402656

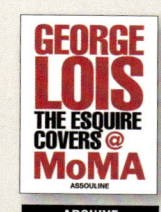

ARCHIVE
GEORGE LOIS
THE ESQUIRE COVERS @ MOMA
ISBN: 9782759404346

ARCHIVE
BRIGHT YOUNG THINGS
ISBN: 9782843232053

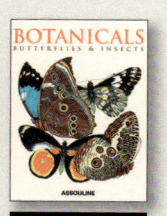

ARCHIVE
BOTANICALS
BUTTERFLIES & INSECTS
ISBN: 9782759402694

ARCHIVE
BERNAR VENET FURNITURE
ISBN: 9782843233302

ARCHIVE
THE BOOK OF THE THOUSAND NIGHTS AND ONE NIGHT FR
ISBN: 9782843237256

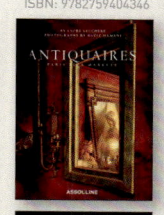

ARCHIVE
ANTIQUAIRES FR
PARIS FLEA MARKETS
ISBN: 9782759404605

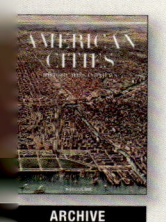

ARCHIVE
AMERICAN CITIES
ISBN: 9782843237164

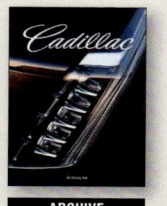

ARCHIVE
CADILLAC
ISBN: 9781614280835

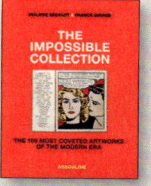

ARCHIVE
THE IMPOSSIBLE COLLECTION
ISBN: 9782759403943

ARCHIVE
INSPIRED STYLES
ISBN: 9782759401642

ARCHIVE
OAKLEY
ISBN: 9781614282686

OTHER FORMATS: ART / DESIGN / ARCHITECTURE CONTINUED

ARCHIVE
MEGALOMANIA FR
TOO MUCH IS NEVER ENOUGH
ISBN: 9782843238949

ARCHIVE
PARIS LIVING ROOMS
ISBN: 9782843233692

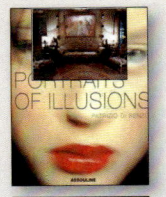

ARCHIVE
PORTRAITS OF ILLUSIONS
ISBN: 9782843236945

ARCHIVE
1000°C DEYROLLE
ISBN: 9782759405589

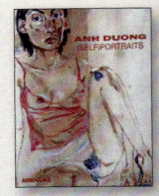

ARCHIVE
ANH DUONG
ISBN: 9782843232855

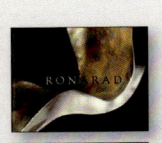

ARCHIVE
RON ARAD
ISBN: 9782843230819

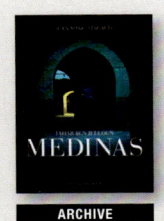

ARCHIVE
MEDINAS
MOROCCO'S HIDDEN CITIES
ISBN: 9782843230516

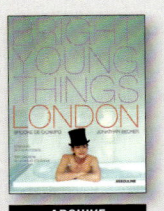

ARCHIVE
BRIGHT YOUNG THINGS LONDON
ISBN: 9782843233371

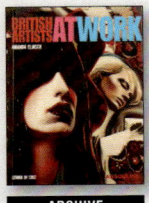

ARCHIVE
BRITISH ARTISTS AT WORK
ISBN: 9782843235054

GENTLEMEN'S COLLECTION

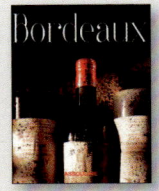

BORDEAUX FR
LEGENDARY WINES
ISBN: 9781614282600
$85 – €85 – £60

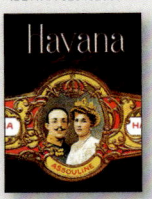

HAVANA FR
LEGENDARY CIGARS
ISBN: 9781614282266
$85 – €85 – £60

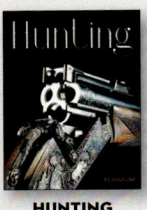

HUNTING
LEGENDARY RIFLES
ISBN: 9781614282617
$85 – €85 – £60

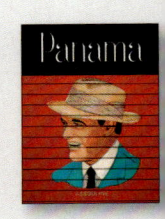

PANAMA FR
LEGENDARY HATS
ISBN: 9781614282259
$85 – €85 – £60

PHOTOGRAPHY

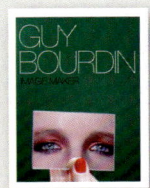

NEW
GUY BOURDIN
IMAGE MAKER
ISBN: 9781614286356
$150 – €150 – £110

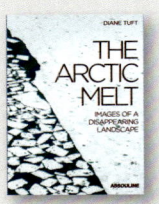

NEW
THE ARCTIC MELT
IMAGES OF A DISAPPEARING LANDSCAPE
ISBN: 9781614285861
$95 – €95 – £70

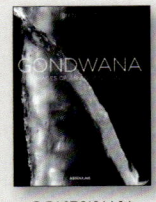

GONDWANA
ISBN: 9781614281993
$95 – €95 – £70

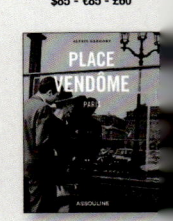

PLACE VENDÔME
ISBN: 9781614282761
$85 – €85 – £60

FERRARI
275 GTB #08011
ISBN: 9781614285281
$95 – €95 – £70

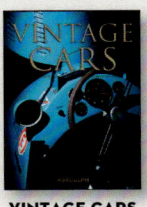

VINTAGE CARS
ISBN: 9781614282624
$95 – €95 – £70

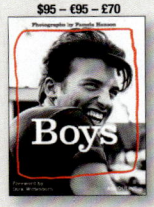

BOYS
ISBN: 9782843238338
$35 – €35 – £28

LE CACA'S CLUB 1984/1994 FR
ISBN: 9782759407507
€150

JONATHAN BECKER
30 YEARS AT VANITY FAIR
ISBN: 9781614280798
$150 – €150 – £110

124

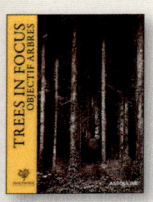

TREES IN FOCUS
ISBN: 9781614281092
$45 - €45 - £35

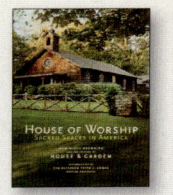

HOUSE OF WORSHIP
SACRED SPACES IN AMERICA
ISBN: 9782843238802
$65 - €65 - £55

JOURNEY OF LIGHT
ISBN: 9781614284703
$125 - €125 - £95

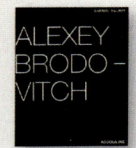

ALEXEY BRODOVITCH (MINI)
ISBN: 9782843237010
$25 - €25 - £18

ARCHIVE
PETER LINDBERGH (MINI)
ISBN: 9782843237034

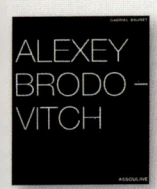

ARCHIVE
ALEXEY BRODOVITCH
ISBN: 9782843233135

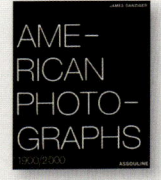

ARCHIVE
AMERICAN PHOTOGRAPHS
ISBN: 9782843231551

ARCHIVE
PETER LINDBERGH
ISBN: 9782843231155

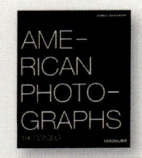

ARCHIVE
AMERICAN PHOTOGRAPHS (MINI)
ISBN: 9782843236990

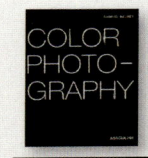

ARCHIVE
COLOR PHOTOGRAPHY (MINI)
ISBN: 9782843236976

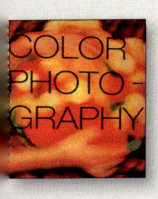

ARCHIVE
COLOR PHOTOGRAPHY
ISBN: 9782843232923

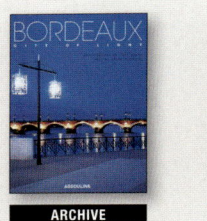

ARCHIVE
BORDEAUX CITY OF LIGHT FR
ISBN: 9782759402847

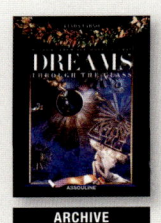

ARCHIVE
DREAMS THROUGH THE GLASS
ISBN: 9782843235221

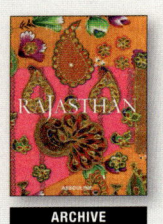

ARCHIVE
RAJASTHAN
ISBN: 9782843234460

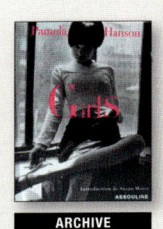

ARCHIVE
GIRLS
ISBN: 9782843231872

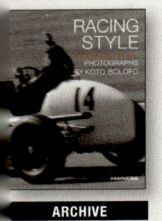

ARCHIVE
RACING STYLE
ISBN: 9782843236815

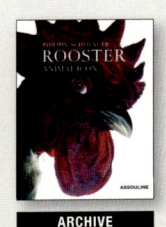

ARCHIVE
ROOSTER
ISBN: 9782843237416

ARCHIVE
OLIVIER THEYSKENS THE OTHER SIDE OF THE PICTURE
ISBN: 9782759404353

ARCHIVE
PAUL HIMMEL
ISBN: 9782843231537

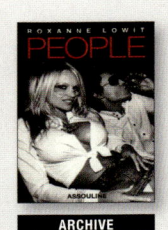

ARCHIVE
PEOPLE LIFE AFTER DARK
ISBN: 9782843232862

ARCHIVE
AHAE: CHÂTEAU DE VERSAILLES FR
ISBN: 9781614281559

ARCHIVE
AHAE: THROUGH MY WINDOW FR
ISBN: 9781614280712

ARCHIVE
SERGE LUTENS FR
ISBN: 9782843230660

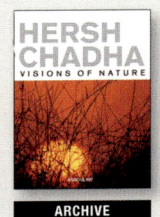

ARCHIVE
HERSH CHADHA VISIONS OF NATURE
ISBN: 9782957402632

ARCHIVE
WOMEN IN ART FIGURES OF INFLUENCE
ISBN: 9781614280811

OTHER FORMATS: PHOTOGRAPHY CONTINUED

ARCHIVE
LUXURY OF SPACE
ISBN: 9782843235214

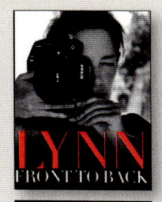

ARCHIVE
LYNN
FRONT TO BACK
ISBN: 9782843235764

ARCHIVE
ORO PLATA
ISBN: 9782843230356

ARCHIVE
FACELESS
ISBN: 9782843232398

COOKING AND TRAVEL

NEW
ASHFORD CASTLE
ISBN: 9781614286172
$95 - €95 - £70

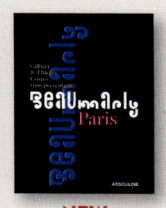

NEW
BEAUMARLY PARIS FR
ISBN: 9781614281665
$75 - €70 - £50

NEW
ETERNALLY RITZ FR
ISBN: 9781614285984
$85 - €85 - £60

LA CUCINA DI LUC FANTIN
BY BULGARI
ISBN: 9781614285243
$150 - €150 - £110

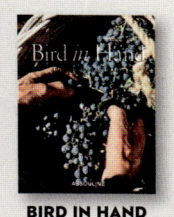

BIRD IN HAND
ADELAIDE HILLS, AUSTRALIA
ISBN: 9781614285410
$95 - €95 - £70

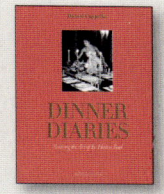

DINNER DIARIES
ISBN: 9781614282044
$50 - €50 - £38

THE WINE QUESTIONNAIRE FR
ISBN: 9781614280514
$50 - €50 - £38

FINE WINES FR
ISBN: 9782759404155
$50 - €50 - £38

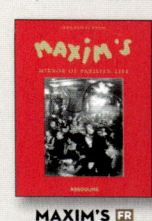

MAXIM'S FR
MIRROR OF PARISIAN LI
ISBN: 9782759405312
$85 - €85 - £60

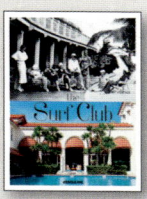

THE SURF CLUB
ISBN: 9781614281795
$75 - €75 - £58

HÔTEL PLAZA ATHÉNÉE FR
ISBN: 9781614282129
$85 - €85 - £60

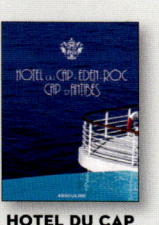

HOTEL DU CAP EDEN ROC FR
CAP D'ANTIBES
ISBN: 9782759401116
$65 - €65 - £55

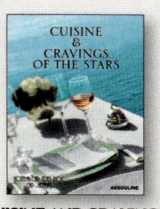

CUISINE AND CRAVINGS OF THE STARS FR
ISBN: 9782759402670
$65 - €65 - £55

LA COLOMBE D'O FR
ISBN: 9782908228472
$85 - €85 - £60

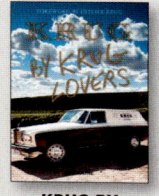

KRUG BY KRUG LOVERS
ISBN: 9781614282884
$75 - €75 - £58

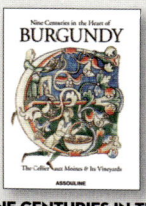

NINE CENTURIES IN THE HEART OF BURGUNDY
FR THE CELLIER AUX MOINES AND ITS VINEYARDS
ISBN: 9781614281405
$85 - €85 - £60

SIMPLY ITALIAN
CLASSIC RECIPES FROM HARRY'S BAR IN VENICE
ISBN: 9781614281610
$50 - €50 - £38

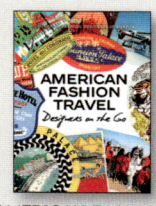

AMERICAN FASHION TRAVEL
ISBN: 9782759405091
$50 - €50 - £38

AMERICAN FASHIO COOKBOOK
ISBN: 9782759404056

ARCHIVE
THE ARTISANS OF PARADISE FR
ISBN: 9782759403981

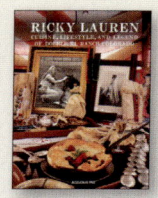

ARCHIVE
RICKY LAUREN
ISBN: 9782843238833

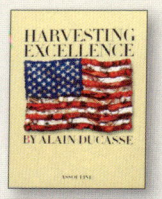

ARCHIVE
HARVESTING EXCELLENCE FR
ISBN: 9782843231919

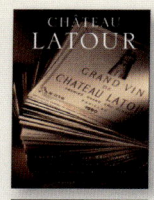

ARCHIVE
CHÂTEAU LATOUR
ISBN: 9782843231001

ARCHIVE
PROVENCE OF ALAIN DUCASSE FR
ISBN: 9782843232473

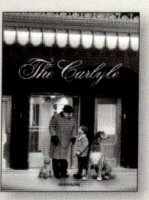

ARCHIVE
THE CARLYLE
ISBN: 9782759401659

ARCHIVE
AMERICA LATINA
ISBN: 9782843233357

ARCHIVE
LA MAMOUNIA FR
ISBN: 9782759404940

ARCHIVE
DANIEL BOULUD COCKTAILS & AMUSE-BOUCHES
ISBN: 9781614280026

ARCHIVE
PARIS
ISBN: 9782843236068

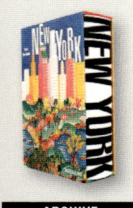

ARCHIVE
NEW YORK
ISBN: 9782843237157

FASHION, BEAUTY, AND JEWELRY

NEW
DIOR BY CHRISTIAN DIOR FR
ISBN: 9781614285489
$195 - €195 - £150

NEW
DIOR BY YVES SAINT LAURENT FR
ISBN: 9781614285991
$195 - €195 - £150

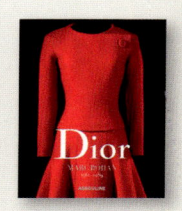

NEW
DIOR BY MARC BOHAN FR
ISBN: 9781614286240
$195 - €195 - £150

NEW
THE ART OF @BARBIESTYLE
ISBN: 9781614285809
$50 - €50 - £38

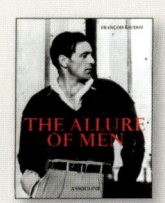

THE ALLURE OF MEN FR
ISBN: 9782843232152
$50 - €50 - £38

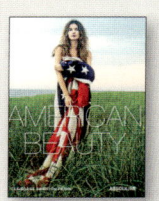

AMERICAN BEAUTY
ISBN: 9781614280507
$75 - €75 - £58

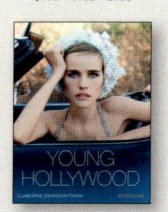

YOUNG HOLLYWOOD
ISBN: 9781614282464
$75 - €75 - £58

DIOR FR
ISBN: 9781614284345
$250 - €250 - £195

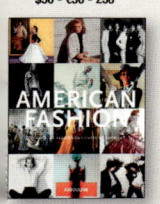

AMERICAN FASHION
ISBN: 9782759401611
$75 - €75 - £58

AMERICAN FASHION ACCESSORIES
ISBN: 9782759402861
$75 - €75 - £58

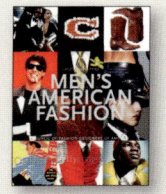

AMERICAN FASHION MENSWEAR
ISBN: 9782759404094
$75 - €75 - £58

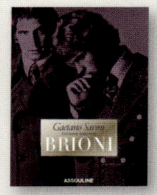

GAETANO SAVINI THE MAN WHO WAS BRIONI
ISBN: 9781614284543
$85 - €85 - £60

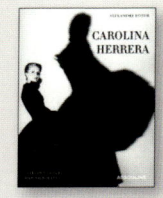

CAROLINA HERRERA
ISBN: 9782843236235
$85 - €85 - £60

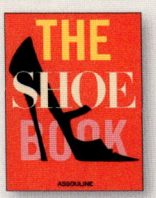

OTHER FORMATS: FASHION, BEAUTY, AND JEWELRY CONTINUED

THE SHOE BOOK
ISBN: 9781614281535
$50 - €50 - £38

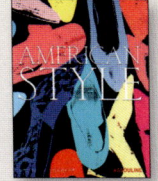

AMERICAN STYLE
ISBN: 9782843236082
$75 - €75 - £58

BRAZILIAN STYLE
ISBN: 9781614280132
$75 - €75 - £58

FRENCH STYLE FR
ISBN: 9781614280996
$75 - €75 - £58

RUSSIAN STYLE FR
ISBN: 9782759403950
$75 - €75 - £58

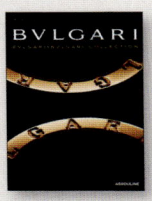

BULGARI: BULGARI-BULGARI COLLECTION FR
ISBN: 9781614281641
$120 - €120 - £95

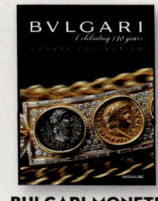

BULGARI MONETE COLLECTION FR
ISBN: 9781614282280
$120 - €120 - £95

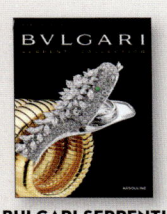

BULGARI SERPENTI COLLECTION FR
ISBN: 9781614280903
$120 - €120 - £95

SHIATZY CHEN
ISBN: 9781614281474
$125 - €125 - £95

AKRIS
ISBN: 9781614280569
$125 - €125 - £95

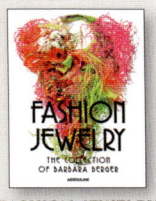

FASHION JEWELRY
THE COLLECTION OF BARBARA BERGER
ISBN: 9781614281061
$75 - €75 - £58

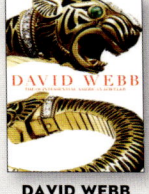

DAVID WEBB
THE QUINTESSENTIAL AMERICAN JEWELER
ISBN: 9781614281511
$85 - €85 - £60

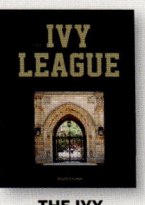

THE IVY LEAGUE
ISBN: 9781614280095
$65 - €65 - £50

SKIN FR
ISBN: 9782759406418
$75 - €75 - £58

RADICAL RENAISSANCE 55+5
ISBN: 9781614285076
$150 - €150 - £110

ARCHIVE
AMERICAN FASHION
SLIPCASE SET OF 2
ISBN: 9781614281337

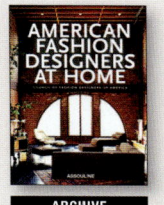

ARCHIVE
AMERICAN FASHION DESIGNERS AT HOME
ISBN: 9782759404711

ARCHIVE
JUDITH RIPKA
BY JUDITH
ISBN: 9781614280170

ARCHIVE
DE BEERS FR
ISBN: 9782759405107

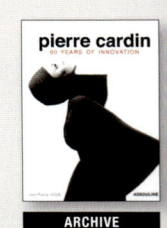

ARCHIVE
PIERRE CARDIN FR
60 YEARS OF INNOVATION
ISBN: 9782759404247

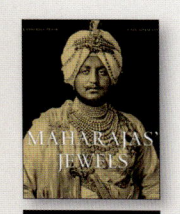

ARCHIVE
MAHARAJAS' JEWELS FR
ISBN: 9782843232183

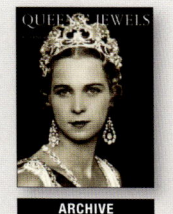

ARCHIVE
QUEENS' JEWELS FR
ISBN: 9782843233647

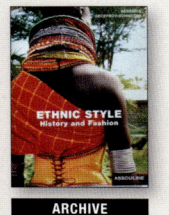

ARCHIVE
ETHNIC STYLE
HISTORY & FASHION
ISBN: 9782843232909

ARCHIVE
THE NEW ENGLISH DANDY
Not available in the UK
ISBN: 9782843237560

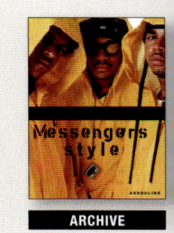

ARCHIVE
MESSENGERS STYLE
ISBN: 9782843237107

21

ARCHIVE
COSTUME NATIONAL
ISBN: 9782759401697

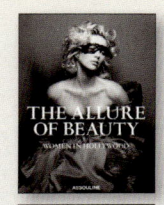

ARCHIVE
THE ALLURE OF BEAUTY
WOMEN IN HOLLYWOOD
ISBN: 9782759402892

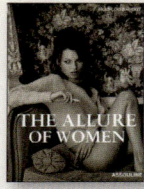

ARCHIVE
THE ALLURE OF WOMEN FR
ISBN: 9782843232886

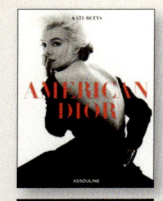

ARCHIVE
AMERICAN DIOR
ISBN: 9782759404872

ARCHIVE
HIDDEN UNDERNEATH FR
ISBN: 9782843236853

ARCHIVE
ULTIMATE STYLE
THE BEST OF THE BEST DRESSED LIST
ISBN: 9782843235139

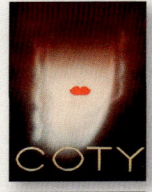

ARCHIVE
COTY FR
ISBN: 9782843236228

ARCHIVE
THE FASHION QUESTIONNAIRE FR
ISBN: 9782759402717

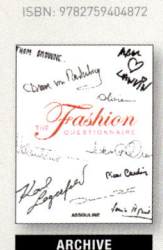

ARCHIVE
THE FASHION QUESTIONNAIRE FR
ISBN: 9782759402731

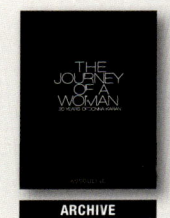

ARCHIVE
THE JOURNEY OF A WOMAN
20 YEARS OF DONNA KARAN
ISBN: 9782843236198

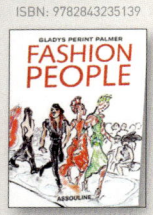

ARCHIVE
FASHION PEOPLE
ISBN: 9782843233623

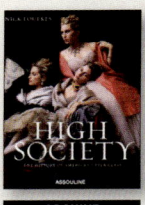

ARCHIVE
HIGH SOCIETY
ISBN: 9782759402885

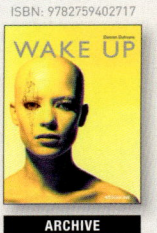

ARCHIVE
WAKE UP
ISBN: 9782843235849

ARCHIVE
MUSIC BY DOLCE & GABBANA
ISBN: 9782843234606

ARCHIVE
HOLLYWOOD BY DOLCE & GABBANA
ISBN: 9782843235269

ARCHIVE
LOUIS VUITTON
THE BUILDING OF LUXURY
ISBN: 9782843236180

ARCHIVE
HUDSON'S BAY COMPANY
ISBN: 9782759405015

ANTHOLOGY COLLECTION
6 x 8.5 in
15.5 x 21.5 cm

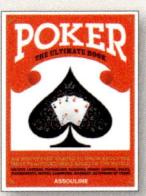

NEW
POKER
THE ULTIMATE BOOK
ISBN: 9781614285533
$50 - €50 - £38

THE TRENCH BOOK
ISBN: 9782759401635
$50 - €50 - £38

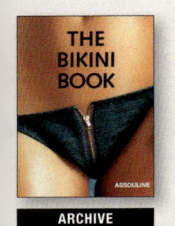

ARCHIVE
THE BIKINI BOOK FR
ISBN: 9782843238253

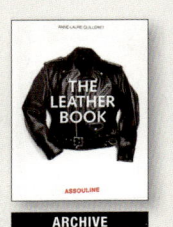

ARCHIVE
THE LEATHER BOOK
ISBN: 9782843235122

ARCHIVE
THE T-SHIRT BOOK
ISBN: 9782843233463

ARCHIVE
RED FR
ISBN: 9782843232220

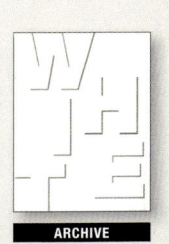

ARCHIVE
WHITE FR
ISBN: 9782843232589

ANTHOLOGY COLLECTION CONTINUED

ARCHIVE
NO SMOKING FR
ISBN: 9782843236167

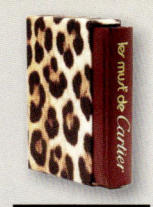

ARCHIVE
LES MUST DE CARTIER FR
ISBN: 9782843234217

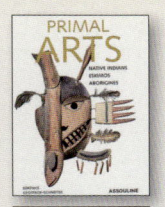

ARCHIVE
PRIMAL ARTS FR
ISBN: 9782843238246

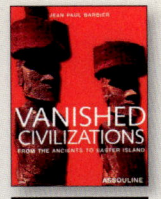

ARCHIVE
VANISHED CIVILIZATIONS
ISBN: 9782843232466

ESSAYS

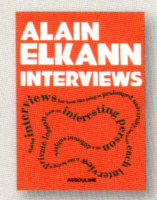

NEW
ALAIN ELKANN INTERVIEWS
ISBN: 9781614286325
$35 - €35 - £28

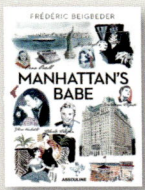

MANHATTAN'S BABE
AN ILLUSTRATED NOVEL
ISBN: 9781614285540
$35 - €35 - £28

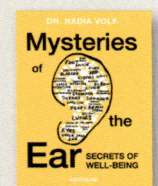

MYSTERIES OF THE EAR
SECRETS OF WELL-BEING FR
ISBN: 9781614284642
$35 - €35 - £28

THE BEE AND THE ACORN
A MEMOIR BY PAULA SUSAN WALLACE
ISBN: 9781614285083
$35 - €35 - £28

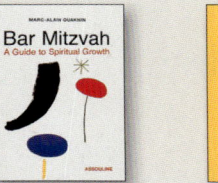

BAR MITZVAH FR
A GUIDE TO SPIRITUAL GROWTH
ISBN: 9782843237188
$25 - €25 - £18

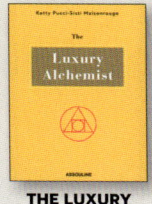

THE LUXURY ALCHEMIST
ISBN: 9781614281504
$35 - €35 - £28

PICASSO FR
THE LAST YEARS
ISBN: 9782843236136
$25 - €25 - £18

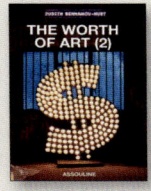

THE WORTH OF ART (2)
ISBN: 9782759401475
$25 - €25 - £18

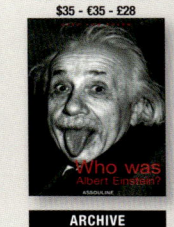

ARCHIVE
WHO WAS ALBERT EINSTEIN?
ISBN: 9782843236730

ARCHIVE
SOMETHING TO HOLD
ISBN: 9782843236846

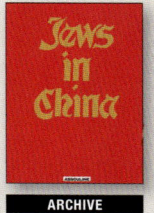

ARCHIVE
JEWS IN CHINA
ISBN: 9782759402854

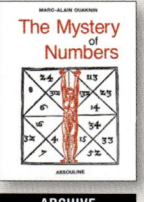

ARCHIVE
THE MYSTERY OF NUMBERS FR
ISBN: 9782843236327

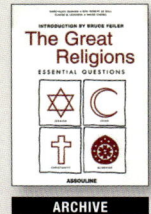

ARCHIVE
THE GREAT RELIGIONS
ESSENTIAL QUESTIONS
ISBN: 9782843236112

2017-2018 COLLECTION

#Carlos's Places *114*
1000° C: Deyrolle *124*

A
ABCDCS David Collins Studio *122*
Africa Is in Style *116*
Ahae: Château de Versailles *125*
Ahae: Through My Window *125*
Ai Weiwei *117*
Akris *128*
Alaïa *115*
Alain Elkann Interviews *86, 105, 130*
Alberto Giacometti *118*
Alexandre Reza *107*
Alexey Brodovitch *125*
Allure of Beauty, The *129*
Allure of Men, The *127*
Allure of Women, The *129*
America Latina *127*
American Beauty *127*
American Cities *107, 123*
American Dior *129*
American Fashion *127*
American Fashion Accessories *127*
American Fashion Cookbook *126*
American Fashion Designers at Home *128*
American Fashion Menswear *127*
American Fashion slipcase set *128*
American Fashion Travel *126*
American Hotel Stories *114*
American Photographs *125*
American Style *128*
André Fu *109*
Andy *118*
Andy Warhol: The Impossible Collection *14–17, 104, 106*
Anh Duong *124*
Antiquaires: Paris Flea Markets *123*
Arabian Horses: The World of Ajmal Arabian Stud *107*
Architect of Dreams: La Mode en Images by Olivier Massart *122*
Arctic Melt, The: Images of a Disappearing Landscape *64–65, 104, 124*
Art Game Book *121*

Art House: The Collaboration of Chara Shreyer & Gary Hutton *74, 105, 111*
Art of @BarbieStyle, The *88–89, 105, 127*
Art of Flying, The *109*
Artisans of Paradise, The *127*
Ashford Castle *87, 105, 126*
Asian Art: India, China, Japan *123*
Aspen Style *66–67, 105, 110*
Axel Vervoordt: The Story of a Style *122*

B
Backstage Cirque du Soleil *106, 111*
Bags *116*
Balenciaga *115*
Ballets Russes *107*
Bals: Legendary Costume Balls of the Twentieth Century *108*
Balthus *118*
Bar Mitzvah: A Guide to Spiritual Growth *160*
Barbie *24–25, 104, 106*
Barclay Butera: Living in Style *123*
Bauhaus *118*
Be My Guest *114*
Beaumarly Paris *76, 105, 126*
Bee and the Acorn: A Memoir by Paula Wallace, The *130*
Beken of Cowes *107*
Be Extraordinary: The Spirit of Bentley *51, 104, 108*
Bernar Venet Furniture *123*
Beyond Extravagance: A Royal Collection of Gems and Jewels *109*
BHV Marais *118*
Big Book of Chic by Miles Redd, The *111*
Big Book of the Hamptons, The *111*
Bikini Book, The *129*
Bird in Hand: Adelaide Hills, Australia *126*
Bisazza *119*
Book of the Thousand Nights and One Night, The *123*
Bordeaux: City of Light *125*
Bordeaux: Legendary Wines *124*
Bosphorus Life, The *72–73, 104, 110*
Botanicals: Butterflies and Insects *123*
Boys *124*
Brancusi New York: 1913–2013 *122*

131

Brancusi Photographs *118*
Brazilian Style *128*
Bright Young Things *123*
Bright Young Things London *124*
British Artists at Work *124*
Buccellati *120*
Bulgari: Bulgari-Bulgari Collection *128*
Bulgari: Bulgari Monete Collection *128*
Bulgari: Serpenti Collection *128*
Bulgari: The Joy of Gems *32–35, 104, 108*

C

Cabinet de Curiosités, Le *121*
Caca's Club, Le *124*
Cacharel: Le Liberty *116*
Cadillac *123*
Canada Goose: Greatness Is Out There *50, 104, 108*
Candy *120*
Carlyle, The *127*
Cartier *119*
Cartier, Les Must de *130*
Cartier Panthère *108*
Carolina Herrera *127*
Catherine Malandrino *115*
Cecil Beaton: The Art of the Scrapbook *108*
Celebrity Cocktails *112*
Cézanne in Provence *117*
Chanel slipcase set *98–99, 115*
Charles James *116*
Charlotte Moss: A Flair for Living *123*
Charlotte Olympia *104, 108*
Charlotte Perriand *118*
Château Latour *127*
Chaumet (Place Vendôme, Tiaras, Naturalism) slipcase set *119*
Chaumet (Photography, Arts, Fêtes) slipcase set *98–99, 105, 119*
Chef Daniel Boulud *115*
Chema Madoz *118*
Chic Stays: Condé Nast Traveller's Favourite People on Their Favourite Places *77, 105, 110*
Chloé *115*
Christofle *119*
Christie's Guide to Jewellery *119*
Cigar Style *120*
Coach *116*

Coca-Cola *122*
Coca-Cola slipcase set *120*
Cocktail Chameleon *94–95, 105, 112*
Cocktails *120*
Codognato *119*
Color Photography *121*
Collection Privée Christian Dior, La *110*
Colombe d'Or, La *126*
Compendium of Interior Styles *123*
Condé Nast Traveler Photographs: 25th Anniversary Collection *111*
Condé Nast Traveler: Room with a View *111*
Condé Nast Traveler: Where Are You? *111*
Corbusier, Le *119*
Costume National *129*
Costumes of Light *115*
Coty *129*
Courrèges *115*
Cova *97, 103, 112*
Craft Cocktails *112*
Creative Tables *112*
Cross Purpose *109*
Cucina di Luca Fantin by Bulgari, La *126*
Cuff Links *116*
Cuisine and Cravings of the Stars *126*

D

Dada Spirit, The *117*
Daniel Boulud Cocktails & Amuse-Bouches *120, 127*
David Webb: The Quintessential American Jeweler *128*
De Beers *128*
De Grisogono: Daring Creativity *46–47, 104, 108*
Diane von Furstenberg: The Wrap *115*
Diego Giacometti *118*
Dinh Van *119*
Dinner Diaries: Reviving the Art of the Hostess Book *126*
Dinner with Georgia O'Keeffe *85, 105, 112*
Dinner with Jackson Pollock *84, 105, 112*
Dior (large format) *127*
Dior (Mémoire) *116*
Dior by Christian Dior *40–41, 104, 127*
Dior by Marc Bohan *40–41, 43, 104, 127*
Dior by Yves Saint Laurent *40–42, 104, 127*
Dior slipcase set *98–99, 115*
Dolce & Gabbana *116*

Dolce Vita Style *114*
Domestic Art: Curated Interiors *122*
Donald *56–61, 104, 110*
Donna Karan *117*
Dreams: Through the Glass *125*
Dressing for the Dark: From the Silver Screen to the Red Carpet *114*
Dressing in the Dark *114*

E

Eames *118*
Egypt Game Book *121*
Eileen Gray *118*
Elie Saab (large format) *108*
Elie Saab (Mémoire) *115*
Emilio Pucci *116*
Empty the Mind: The Art of Park Seo-Bo *123*
Enoc Perez *123*
Escape Hotel Stories *114*
Eternally Ritz *83, 105, 126*
Ethiopian Highlands *109*
Ethnic Style: History and Fashion *128*

F

Faceless *126*
Farfetch Curates Art *117*
Farfetch Curates Design *118*
Farfetch Curates Food *120*
Fashion & Surrealism *117*
Fashion Dogs *116*
Fashion Game Book *121*
Fashion Jewelry: The Collection of Barbara Berger *128*
Fashion People *128*
Fashion Questionnaire, The *129*
Fayum *118*
Fendi Roma *108*
Fernand Léger: A Survey of Iconic Works *106*
Fernando Botero *28–29, 104, 106*
Ferrari: 275 GTB #08011 *124*
Fig & Olive: Cuisine of the French Riviera *112*
Fine Wines *126*
Flowers: Art & Bouquets *110*
Food & Life *112*
Fornasetti *119*
Fred Astaire Style *116*
Fred Joaillier *108*
French Riviera *114*
French Riviera in the 1920s, The *108*
French Style *128*
Frida Kahlo: Fashion as the Art of Being *108*

G

Gaetano Savini: The Man Who Was Brioni *127*
Gaia *106, 107, 111*
Gandhara *118*
Gauguin Noa Noa *118*
Geishas *117*
Geoffrey Beene *114*
George Lois: On His Creation of the Big Idea *123*
George Lois: The *Esquire* Covers @ MoMA *123*
Giacobetti *75, 105, 110*
Girls *125*
Glass House, The *119*
Golden Menagerie, The *108*
Golf: The Impossible Collection *18–21, 104, 106*
Gondwana *124*
Gottex *116*
GQ Men *109*
Grand Bazaar Istanbul, The *109*
Great Religions: Essential Questions, The *130*
Greek Beauty *118*
Grès *116*
Gruau *116*
Gruau: Portraits of Men *111*
Guerlain *116*
Guy Bourdin: Image Maker *62–63, 104, 124*
Gypset Living *113*
Gypset Style *113*
Gypset Travel *113*
Gypset slipcase set *113*

H

H.Stern (large format) *108*
H.Stern (Mémoire) *119*
Haggadah *109*
Hair *110*
Hamptons Gardens *109*
Happy Times *113*
Harry Winston *119*
Harvesting Excellence *127*
Havana: Legendary Cigars *124*
Helena Rubinstein *116*
Henry T. Segerstrom *123*
Hersh Chadha: Visions of Nature *125*

Hidden Collection, The *26, 104, 106*
Hidden Underneath *129*
High Society *129*
Hitchcock Style *114*
Hollywood by Dolce & Gabbana *129*
Hotel du Cap: Eden Roc Cap d'Antibes *126*
Hôtel Plaza Athénée *126*
Hotel Stories *114*
House of Worship: Sacred Spaces in America *125*
Hudson's Bay Company *129*
Hunting: Legendary Rifles *124*
Hyundai: Live Brilliant *107*

I

Ibiza Bohemia *68–69, 106, 110*
Impossible Collection, The *106, 123*
Impossible Collection of Cars, The *106*
Impossible Collection of Design, The *106*
Impossible Collection of Fashion, The *106*
Impossible Collection of Jewelry, The *106*
Impossible Collection of Motorcycles, The *106*
Impossible Collection of Watches, The *106*
Impossible Collection of Wine, The *22–23, 104, 106*
In the Spirit of Aspen *113*
In the Spirit of Bali *112*
In the Spirit of Beverly Hills *113*
In the Spirit of Cannes *114*
In the Spirit of Capri *113*
In the Spirit of Gstaad *112*
In the Spirit of Harlem *113*
In the Spirit of Las Vegas *113*
In the Spirit of Miami Beach *113*
In the Spirit of Monte Carlo *113*
In the Spirit of Napa Valley *113*
In the Spirit of New Orleans *113*
In the Spirit of Palm Beach *113*
In the Spirit of Rio *112*
In the Spirit of Seville *113*
In the Spirit of St. Barths *113*
In the Spirit of St. Tropez *113*
In the Spirit of the Hamptons *113*
In the Spirit of Venice *113*
Indian Beauty *114*
Insects *121*
Inspired Styles *123*
Island Hotel Stories *115*

Italian Dream, The: Wine, Heritage, Soul *78–79, 105, 110*
Ivy League, The *128*

J

J. M. Frank *118*
Jacques Fath *116*
Jean Cocteau *118*
Jean-Louis Scherrer *116*
Jean-Michel Frank *38–39, 104, 108*
Jean Paul Gaultier *115*
Jean-Paul Hévin *120*
Jewels of the Renaissance *108*
Jews in China *130*
Jonathan Becker: 30 Years at Vanity Fair *124*
Journey by Design: Katharine Pooley *87, 105, 110*
Journey of a Woman: 20 Years of Donna Karan, The *129*
Journey of Light *125*
Juan Pablo Molyneux: At Home *122*
Judith Ripka by Judith *128*

K

Keiichi Tahara: Light, Sculpture, Photography *123*
Kennedys slipcase set, The *120*
Kiss the Past Hello: 100 Years of the Coca-Cola Contour Bottle *124*
Klimt & Fashion *117*
Krug by Krug Lovers *122*

L

Lanvin *116*
Last Heroes: A Tribute to the Olympic Games *121*
Lautrec in Paris *117*
Lee *113*
Léon Hatot *119*
Leather Book, The *129*
Life as a Visitor *114*
Life of Style *109*
Light of Series slipcase set, The *110*
Light of Istanbul, The *110*
Light of London, The *109*
Light of Jerusalem, The *110*
Light of New York, The *109*
Light of Paris, The *109*
Light of Tokyo, The *110*
Light of Venice, The *110*
Little Black Dress, The *115*

Little Black Dress Diet, The *117*
Living Architecture: Greatest American Houses
   of the 20th Century *111*
Living Next to Delphi: Ancient Inspirations,
   Contemporary Interiors *122*
Lladró *119*
Loris Azzaro *115*
Lost Africa *121*
Lost Divas *123*
Lost Fish *122*
Louis Vuitton: The Building of Luxury *129*
Louis Vuitton: Icons *115*
Louis Vuitton Windows *106*
Louvre Game Book *121*
Lovers by Peynet *117*
Luxury Alchemist, The *130*
Luxury Collection Certified Indigenous, The *113*
Luxury Collection Destination Guides, The *107*
Luxury Collection Epicurean Journeys, The *107, 113*
Luxury Collection Global Epicurean, The *92, 105, 112*
Luxury Collection Hotel Stories, The *113*
Luxury Collection Room with a View, The *107, 113*
Luxury of Space *126*
Lynn: Front to Back *126*

M

Magritte: The Empire of Images *107*
Maharajas' Jewels *128*
Mamounia, La *127*
Mandarin Oriental *109*
Manhattan's Babe *130*
Manolo Valdés *122*
Manolo Valdés: Monumental Sculpture
   at the New York Botanical Garden *122*
Manolo Valdés: Place Vendôme *105, 122*
Marc Jacobs *115*
Maria by Callas: In Her Own Words *44–45, 104, 108*
María Félix: La Doña *120*
Marie-Antoinette Style *120*
Marilyn *120*
Marvin Traub: Like No Other Career *114*
Masks *121*
Mattel: 70 Years *122*
Maxim's: Mirror of Parisian Life *126*
MCM *116*
Medinas: Morocco's Hidden Cities *124*

Megalomania *124*
Messengers Style *128*
Messika *119*
Michele Bönan *111*
Mikimoto *119*
Miller House and Garden *119*
Miró's Studio *117*
Modern Views: An Homage to Mies van der Rohe
   and Philip Johnson *111*
Mona Lisa *117*
Morris Lapidus *118*
Moulin Rouge *120*
Music by Dolce & Gabbana *129*
Movie Game Book *121*
Music Game Book *121*
Mysteries of the Ear: Secrets of Well-Being *130*
Mystery of Numbers, The *130*

N

Nancy Gonzalez *116*
Nardi *109*
New English Dandy, The *128*
New York *127*
Night Before: BAFTA, The *114*
Nine Centuries in the Heart of Burgundy:
   The Cellier aux Moines and Its Vineyards *126*
No Smoking *130*
Nomad Deluxe *110*

O

Oakley *123*
Olivier Theyskens: The Other Side of The Picture *125*
Once Weddings *106*
One of 100: Maserati and Zegna *109*
Orient Express: Origins of the Art of Travel *110*
Oro Plata *126*
Oscar de la Renta *109*
Oscar Niemeyer *119*
Ottoman Chic *111*

P

Palais Bulles, The *122*
Palm Springs Style *115*
Panama: Legendary Hats *124*
Paris *127*
Paris Hotel Stories *115*
Paris in the 1920s with Kiki de Montparnasse *109*
Paris Living Rooms *124*

Paul Himmel *125*
Pearl Necklace, The *110*
Peggy Guggenheim *117*
Penny: A Little History of Luck, The *120*
Penthouse Special Edition *107*
People: Life After Dark *125*
Peter Lindbergh *123*
Philip Treacy *116*
Philippe Ferrandis *119*
Picabia *117*
Picasso: The Last Years *130*
Picasso: The Objects *117*
Pierre Cardin *36–37, 104, 108*
Pierre Cardin: 60 Years of Innovation *128*
Pierre Paulin *118*
Pioneers of the Possible *114*
Place Vendôme *124*
Planets *121*
Pliage by Longchamp, Le *115*
Poiret *116*
Poker: The Ultimate Book *100–101, 105, 129*
Polo Games, The *120*
Polo: The Nomadic Tribe *122*
Portraits and Caftans of the Ottoman Sultans *122*
Portraits of Illusions *124*
Portraits of the New Architecture *111*
Portraits of the New Architecture 2 *111*
Portraits of the Renaissance *122*
Primal Arts *130*
Private: Giancarlo Giammetti *109*
Provence of Alain Ducasse *127*
Proust Questionnaire, The *122*
Privileged Life: Celebrating Wasp Style, A *114*
Puig: 100 Years of a Family Business *111*
Putman Style *114*

Q

Queens' Jewels *128*
Queen's People, The *107*

R

Racing Style *125*
Radical Renaissance 55+5 *128*
Rajasthan *125*
Rajasthan Style *107, 111*
Raymond Loewy *119*
Rebel Style *116*

Red *129*
Reflections: In Conversation with Today's Artists by Matt Black *74, 105, 110*
Renzo Mongiardino: Renaissance Master of Style *122*
Ricky Lauren *127*
Robert Indiana *116*
Roberto Cavalli *117*
Roger Vivier *115*
Ron Arad *124*
Rooster *125*
Roy Soleil, Le *122*
Royal Holidays *115*
Ruffian: Inside Out *117*
Russian Style *128*

S

Sade *122*
Santiago Calatrava *106*
Santiago Calatrava: Oculus *70–71, 104, 110*
Sculptures of Picasso, The *121*
School of Fashion, The: 30 Parsons Designers *114*
Serge Lutens *125*
Sergio Rossi *117*
Sevan Biçakçi *109*
Sevan Biçakçi: Time *52, 104, 108*
Sex Game Book *121*
Shiatzy Chen *128*
Shinde Jewels *119*
Shoe Book, The *128*
Simply Italian by Cipriani *126*
Skin *128*
Smoke & Fire: Recipes and Menus for Entertaining Outdoors *112*
So Far So Goude *122*
Solstiss *117*
Something to Hold *130*
South Pole *107*
Stephan Weiss: Connecting the Dots *123*
Studio *121*
Surf Club, The *126*
Suzanne Syz: Art Jewels *109*
Swans: Legends of the Jet Society *108*
Symbols of Catholicism *120*
Symbols of Freemasonry *120*
Symbols of Islam *120*
Symbols of Judaism *120*

Symbols of Tibetan Buddhism *120*

T

Tennis Fashion *117*
Tequila Cocktails *112*
Ties *117*
Tim Palen: Photographs from *The Hunger Games* *111*
Time by Chanel *114*
To India With Love: From New York to Mumbai *114*
Topolino *117*
Touch of Style, A *111*
Transform: 60 Makeup Looks by Toni Malt *96, 105, 112*
Travels with Chufy: Confidential Destinations by Sofía Sanchez de Betak *93, 105, 112*
Trees in Focus *125*
Trench Book, The *129*
T-Shirt Book, The *129*

U

Ultimate Style: The Best of the Best Dressed List *129*
Unexpected Creations by Lotus Arts de Vivre *108*

V

Valentino: At the Emperor's Table *108*
Valentino: Mirabilia Romae *108*
Van Cleef & Arpels *119*
Vanished Civilizations *130*
Vatican *123*
Venetian Chic *87, 105, 110*
Venice Synagogues *106*
Veruschka *107*
Veuve Clicquot *110*
Video Game Art *121*
Vienna 1900 *118*
Vintage Cars *124*
Vintage Cocktails *112*
Visionary Women *114*
Volez, Voguez, Voyagez by Louis Vuitton Malletier *114*

W

Wake Up *129*
Watches: The Ultimate Guide *114*
Well-Lived Life, The *123*
When Art Meets Design *111*
White *129*
Who Was Albert Einstein? *130*
Windows at Bergdorf Goodman *107*

Wine Questionnaire, The *126*
Women in Art: Figures of Influence *125*
World of Departures, The *111*
Worth of Art (2), The *130*

Y

Yellow: Veuve Clicquot *120*
Yohji Yamamoto *117*
Young Hollywood *127*
Yves Saint Laurent *115*

Z

Zadora Timepieces *120*

EXCLUSIVE ASSOULINE BOUTIQUES

AMERICAS

ASSOULINE NEW YORK - THE PLAZA HOTEL
The Plaza Hotel, Mezzanine
768 Fifth Avenue
New York, NY 10019, USA
+1 212 593 7236
newyork@assouline.com

ASSOULINE NEW YORK - THE MARK HOTEL
25 East 77th Street (at Madison Avenue)
New York, NY 10075, USA
+1 212 606 3155
markhotel@assouline.com

ASSOULINE NEW YORK - D&D BUILDING
979 Third Avenue
New York, NY 10022, USA
+1 212 888 0199
helen@assouline.com

ASSOULINE COSTA MESA - SOUTH COAST PLAZA
Level 1 - Jewel Court
3333 Bristol Street
Costa Mesa, CA 92626, USA
+1 714 557 1882
southcoastplaza@assouline.com

ASSOULINE PACIFIC DESIGN CENTER
8687 Melrose Ave. G-154
West Hollywood, CA 90069
assoulinepdc@assouline.com

ASSOULINE PALM BEACH (OCTOBER 2017)
Royal Poinciana Plaza
340 Royal Poinciana Way
Palm Beach FL 33480
Palmbeach@assouline.com

ASSOULINE LIMA
Avenida Santa Cruz 970
Miraflores, Lima, Peru
+51 1213 5114 ext. 271
igierke@gyghome.com

ASSOULINE MEXICO CITY
Calle Newton 35, Colonia Polanco
Delegación Miguel Hidalgo
11560 México, D.F., Mexico
+52 55 5281 0568
marcela@aeditores.com

EUROPE

ASSOULINE LONDON - MAISON ASSOULINE
196a Piccadilly, Mayfair
W1J 9EY London, UK
+44 203 327 9370
piccadilly@assouline.com

ASSOULINE PARIS
35 rue Bonaparte
75006 Paris, France
+33 1 43 29 23 20
paris@assouline.com

ASSOULINE PARIS - LE BON MARCHÉ
115 rue du Bac
75007 Paris, France
+33 1 71 37 85 55
lebonmarche@assouline.com

ASSOULINE ISTANBUL - BEBEK
Cevdet Pasa Cad No 25A
Bebek, Istanbul 34342, Turkey
+90 212 287 5534
istanbul@assouline.com.tr

ASSOULINE ISTANBUL - ZORLU CENTER
Beymen Home - Zorlu Center
Zincirlikuyu, Istanbul 34340, Turkey
+90 212 306 33 00
zorlu@assouline.com.tr

ASSOULINE VENICE - BAUER HOTEL
San Marco, 1455
30124 Venice, Italy
+39 041 240 6876
venezia@assouline.com

ASSOULINE ROME - CHEZ DÉDÉ
Via di Monserrato, 35
00186 Rome, Italy
+39 06 8377 2934

ASSOULINE PORTUGAL
JNCQUOI
Avenida da Liberdade - Nº 182 / 184
1250 - 146 Lisboa
Portugal

ASSOULINE BRUSSELS
Rue Lebeau, 65
Brussels 1000, Belgium
+32479451202
kathleen@alaskas.be

ASIA

ASSOULINE SEOUL
Jumyung Building
Sinsa-dong 631-36, Gangnam-Gu
Seoul 135-895, South Korea
+82 2 517 0316
info@assouline.co.kr

MIDDLE EAST

ASSOULINE DUBAI
MAISON ASSOULINE
The Dubai Mall (march 2018)
Financial Centre Road
Downtown Dubai
United Arab Emirates

EXCLUSIVE SHOP-IN-SHOPS

BOOKS & BOOKS, BAL HARBOUR
9700 Collins Avenue, Suite 370
Bal Harbour, FL 33154, USA
+1 305 864 4241
marck@booksandbooks.com

BOOKS & BOOKS, CORAL GABLES
265 Aragon Avenue
Coral Gables, FL 33134, USA
+1 305 442 4408
cathy@booksandbooks.com

BOOKS & BOOKS, MIAMI BEACH
927 Lincoln Road
Miami Beach, FL 33139, USA
+1 305 532 3222
nalani@booksandbooks.com

FORTY FIVE TEN, DALLAS
4510 McKinney Avenue
Dallas, TX 75205, USA
+1 214 559 4510

LA TABLE, HOUSTON
1800 Post Oak Boulevard, #6110
Houston, TX 77056, USA
+1 713 439 1000

HEADQUARTERS

USA / NEW YORK
3 Park Avenue
27th Floor
New York, NY 10016
+1 212 989 6769
+1 212 647 0005

RETAIL
retail@assouline.com

WHOLESALE
wholesale@assouline.com

PR, EVENTS & PARTNERSHIPS
press@assouline.com
assouline@prconsulting.net (U.S. only)

EDITORIAL
editorial@assouline.com

CUSTOMER SERVICE
customerservice@assouline.com

DIGITAL MARKETING
digital@assouline.com

PHOTO CREDITS

All images © Assouline except: cover and pages 58–61: © Donald Robertson; pages 2, 4-7, 42-43, 53, 82: © Laziz Hamani; page 3: © Emilia Brandão/Vogue Brazil/Edições Globo Condé Nast; page 18: © Kevin Murray; page 20 (clockwise from top left): © Sotheby's, © Patrick O'Brien, courtesy Kiawah Island Golf Resort, © Craig Hanson/Shutterstock, © John Paul, courtesy Royal Dornoch Golf Club; page 21: © George Grantham Bain Collection, Library of Congress Prints and Photographs Division Washington, DC; page 25: © Mattel; page 26: © Abedin Taherkenareh/Epa/REX/Shutterstock; page 27: © The Metropolitan Museum of Art/Art Resource, NY; page 28 (clockwise from top left): © Fernando Botero, courtesy Lina Botero (3), © Fernando Botero, courtesy Museo Botero, Banco de la República, Bogotá, Colombia; page 32: © Fabrizio Ferri, model Tatiana Patitz; page 34: © Antonio Barrella, Studio Orizzonte; page 35: © Ellen von Unwerth/Trunk Archive, Bianca Balti @ Brave Models; page 36 (top): © Archives Pierre Cardin; page 37: © Terry O'Neill/Hulton Archive/Getty Images; page 38: All Rights Reserved; page 45 (clockwise from top left): © Studio Sebert, © Roger Picard, courtesy Fonds de Dotation Maria Callas, All Rights Reserved (2), courtesy Frank Abe Collection, All Rights Reserved; page 46: © Imagie; page 50: © Natasha V.; pages 51, 78: © Aline Coquelle; page 52: © Kemal Olça; page 63: © The Guy Bourdin Estate; page 65: © Diane Tuft; page 67 (clockwise from top left): © Simon Upton for Beauty at Home, courtesy AERIN, © Aerin Lauder, © David Johnston Architects, © The St. Regis Aspen Resort; page 68 (clockwise from top left): © Anne Menke (2), © Eugenie Pons, © Petrovsky & Ramone, © Gwen Le Bras, © Maria Simon; page 70 (top left, bottom right): © Alan Karchmer; page 70 (bottom left): © Santiago Calatrava; page 71: © Hufton + Crow; pages 72-73: © Emre Guven; page 76 (clockwise from top left): © Benjamin Loyseau, © Florian Leger, © Matt Guegan, © Yan Céh; page 83: © Robyn Lea; page 87 (lower left): © Ashford Castle; page 93: © Alexandre de Betak; pages 94-95: Eventstyle, LLC; page 96: © Sylvio Kuehn; page 97: © Harald Gottschalk.

Printed in Italy.